THE WHISKIES OF SCOTLAND

"A valuable reprint . . . revised and updated. . . . A definitive reference book and a perfect companion for anyone who enjoys his dram."
—*Aberdeen Evening Express*

This is the fourth edition, revised and enlarged, of R.J.S. McDowall's classic book, which has been an enthusiastic and knowledgeable guide to the whiskies of Scotland for two decades.

An international recession that closed many long-established distilleries, and a shift in drinking habits toward wines, and, paradoxically, toward the single malts, brought about many changes in the whisky industry. Professor McDowall, now in his nineties, felt that few were as well qualified to assess those changes as his son-in-law, William Waugh, who owes perhaps even more to his father-in-law's tutelage than to his fine cellar.

THE WHISKIES OF SCOTLAND is also a reliable guide to those distilleries that encourage visitors. Indeed, it is *the* book for all who are interested in whisky—from the novice, who innocently imagines that all Scotch is created equal, to the better informed, who appreciate the traditional skills that go into producing a distinctive whisky, unique and inimitable.

"Several books on Scotch have been published since Professor McDowall's, but none better, particularly for its emphasis on the single malts."
—*Financial Times*

COVER PHOTOS: *(front)* Laphroaig Distillery, Isle of Islay *(courtesy of Long John International Ltd); (back)* wash stills at Talisker Distillery, Isle of Skye *(courtesy of The Distillers Company plc).*

THE
WHISKIES
OF SCOTLAND,

R.J.S. McDOWALL

/ FOURTH EDITION /
Revised by William Waugh

NEW AMSTERDAM
New York

Title-page vignette reproduced from
The NB: The First Hundred Years by Leslie Gardiner (1985)
by kind permission of The North British Distillery Company Ltd

Fourth revised edition published in the United States by
NEW AMSTERDAM BOOKS/THE MEREDITH PRESS
171 Madison Avenue
New York, N.Y. 10016.

First printing.

Published by arrangement with
John Murray (Publishers) Ltd., London.

Library of Congress Cataloging-in-Publication Data

McDowall, R.J.S. (Robert John Stewart), 1892-
The whiskies of Scotland.

Bibliography: p. 176
Includes index.
1. Whiskey—Scotland.   I. Waugh, William.   II. Title.
TP605.M33   1987   641.2'52'09411   87-21962
ISBN 0-941533-06-9 (pbk.)

Contents

Preface

Professor McDowall wrote the first edition of this book in 1967, after he had retired from the Chair of Physiology at King's College, London, which he had held since 1923. He was able to spend many enjoyable holidays in Scotland during which he visited virtually all the distilleries,. At that time there was a whisky boom, but single malts were not readily available outside Scotland. The first edition (the proceeds from which were given to the Asthma Research Council) was reprinted in 1968; there was a second edition in 1971 and a third (with a supplement) in 1975. The book has been published in the United States and translated into Swedish, German, Spanish and, most recently, Japanese. Its success was a reflection of the author's ability to give a personal account of the pleasures of whisky drinking, together with a readable description of distilleries and the industry in general.

In the last ten years a great deal has happened. The whisky industry, like all others, is in recession and there have been many changes in its organisation. On the other hand, single malt whiskies have become increasingly popular in the UK and worldwide and they are much more readily available than they used to be. Social attitudes have also altered – and so have drinking habits, with a swing towards white spirits and wine. A new edition is needed to take account of these changes; but the author, who is now in his nineties, did not feel able to undertake the task, although he remains fit and well (a tribute to whisky perhaps?).

My own position is somewhat similar to Professor McDowall's in 1967, in the sense that I have just retired from the Chair of Orthopaedic Surgery in the University of Nottingham. Like him, I have no connection with the whisky business, but I am his son-in-law. Whenever my wife and I visited London we stayed with her father, during which time I received much serious tuition and, of more importance, practical experience of whisky. So I share some of his knowledge, and certainly his enjoyment of the drink.

Mac, as he is known to his wide circle of friends, had a very large collection of malts and his discernment is recognised by many serious drinkers. This is well illustrated by a quotation from a paper by Sir James Howie, an eminent microbiologist: 'In 1967 I met a 1952 Macallan, just ready for drinking. It was marvellous. In 1970 I met a Macallan I did not like – nor did my wife. I reported to Professor McDowall. "Not possible," he said, "unless you both have colds, or unless it's 1954." It *was* 1954.' This splendid example of whisky one-upmanship was published in the *British Medical Journal* (24–31 December 1983) and the relevant papers are discussed in Chapter 12.

But although Mac's generous hospitality over the years had given me a liking for whisky, I needed advice and many people in the whisky industry were prepared to correct entries in the last edition or send me literature describing their firm's activities. They are listed separately and it is a pleasure to acknowledge their help. Aside from this I wish to thank Brian Spiller, who had been involved with previous editions and who, on this occasion, was prepared to help again. His meticulous reading and correction of my typescript makes me confident that I have not made any major errors. It is difficult to express my gratitude to him adequately, but without his expert guidance this would have been a different book. On the practical side again, I should also like to thank my old friend James Scott. His wisdom and skill as an orthopaedic surgeon have made him the recipient of much malt whisky from grateful patients. On many occasions he has helped to educate my palate with generous drams of Scotland's most delectable malts. Mac's elder daughter, my wife, helped with typing, so the production of the fourth edition has been very much a family affair. Duncan McAra, of John Murray, has collaborated at every step and his splendid enthusiasm for the book and its subject has provided valuable encouragement and support.

Revision has involved a great deal of rewriting and new chapters have been added to include such topics as Visiting Distilleries; Vatted Malts; and the Whisky Industry Today. Individual single malts and their distilleries are described, but the importance of blended whisky in developing and maintaining the world market is emphasised. Nevertheless the basic structure of the book remains as it was and with it the author's enthusiasm and his critical appraisal of individual whiskies.

William Waugh

ABBREVIATIONS

The following abbreviations are used in the text:

ADP: Amalgamated Distilled Products
DCL: Distillers Company Limited
DSWG: Distilling Sector Working Group
IDV: International Distillers and Vintners
J & B: Justerini & Brooks
lpa: litres of pure alcohol
mla: million litres of alcohol
NB: North British Distillery
PLC: Public Limited Company
SMD: Scottish Malt Distillers
SUITS: Scottish & Universal Investments
SWA: Scotch Whisky Association
UK: United Kingdom
US: United States of America
% vol: percentage alcohol by volume

ACKNOWLEDGEMENTS

The author would like to thank the following individuals who helped, in different ways, by providing information included in the fourth edition: T. B. Ashcroft (John Dewar); A. H. Barclay (Hiram Walker); Terry Brooke (Distillers Co plc); Pamela Brough (Charles Mackinlay); Sue Brown (Macdonald & Muir); Ron Brown (Scotch Whisky Association); John Burns (Invergordon Distillers); Josephine Clarke (Wm. Grant); James Cryle (Matthew Gloag); Anne Dana (Scotch Malt Whisky Society); Peter Doble (IDV); Lesley De Jean (Royal College of Surgeons, Edinburgh); Sue Faldo (Stanley Morrison); Peter Fairley (Glenturret Distillery); A. J. M. Graham (Inver House); George Grant (J. & G. Grant); Anthony Hall (James Buchanan); R. B. Jamieson (John Begg); H. A. Jess (Ainslie & Heilbron); Walter Laidlaw (White Horse); Mark Lawson (Seagram Distillers PLC); Michael Lunn (Whyte & Mackay); I. V. Lockwood (ADP); C. S. McBain (Chivas Bros.); A. J. Macfarlane (Wm. Teacher); A. Macpherson (Allt à Bhainne Distillery); Alan Meikle (Highland Distilleries); Jim Milne (J. & B., Blythswood); Wallace Milroy (Soho Wine Market); Archie Ness (Cardhu Distillery); Oliver Pemberton (Berry Bros. & Rudd); W. H. C. Phillips (Macallan); Simon Richmond (Arthur Bell); Peter Roger; Ian Ross (Macdonald Greenlees); Nigel Shattock (John Walker); Julia Thorold (J. & B.); George Urquhart (Gordon & MacPhail); James Waddel (J. & G. Stewart); John Watson (Wm. Sanderson); I. A. Whyte (House of Campbell); Jeffrey Wormstone (Scotch Whisky Association).

I

An Introduction to Whisky

Wi' tippeny [ale], we fear nae evil;
Wi' usquabae, we'll face the devil!
BURNS, *Tam o' Shanter*

The origin of whisky is hidden in the mists of antiquity. Wine
made from barley was certainly known to the ancient Greeks.
Some think whisky came, like Christianity, to Scotland from
Ireland. This may or may not be so, but certainly it was the
domestic drink of the Highlands of Scotland from very early
times, and was distilled for the households of the chiefs and
their friends. Its name is derived from the Gaelic uisgebeatha,
sometimes written Usqua, or shortened to Usky, meaning the
water of life – an obvious relation of the aqua vitae of many
countries, but of a very different character.

It is customary, in every book written on whisky, to quote the
Scottish Exchequer Rolls of 1494 in which is recorded: 'eight
bolls of malt to Friar John Cor wherewith to make aqua vitae'.
Certainly whisky had already reached the Court of King James
IV of Scotland by the year 1500.

In Edinburgh distilling was such a popular and lucrative
pastime that some attempt was made to control it in 1505 when
the Barbers and Surgeons of the City were given the exclusive
right to make and sell aqua vitae (in this instance, whisky).
When the Barbers and the Surgeons separated in 1772, a decree
forebad the Barbers from practising surgery, but as a compensation they were allowed to continue distilling. The
Surgeons later became the Royal College of Edinburgh.

Holinshed extolled the virtues of whisky as early as 1577 as follows:

Beying moderately taken, sayeth he, it cutteth fleume, it lighteneth the mynd, it quickeneth the spirits, it cureth the hydropsie, it healeth the stranguary, it pounceth the stone, it repelleth gravel, it puffeth away ventositie, it kepyth and preserveth the hed from whyrlying, the eyes from dazelying, the tongue from lispying, the mouthe from snafflying, the teethe from chatterying, the throte from rattlying, the weasan from stieflying, the stomach from womblying, the harte from swellyng, the bellie from wirtching, the guts from rumblying, the hands from shivering, the sinoews from shrinkyng, the veynes from crumplyng, the bones from akying, the marrow from soakyng, and truly it is a sovereign liquor if it be ordlie taken.

In London, the Worshipful Company of Distillers was given powers in 1638 to regulate the Trade of Distillers and others in the City and in the suburbs within 21 miles. Before this time cereals unfit for human consumption were commonly used to make potable spirit; indeed, it would seem that the making of alcohol was a common way of using cereals which had fermented as a result of wet harvests when the grain could not be dried. Some of the whisky in the early days must have been very rough and toxic stuff.

The first tax on whisky was imposed by the Scots Parliament in 1644, possibly in order to raise money to pay the Duke of Montrose's Highland Army to fight in support of King Charles I. Most of the distilling carried out at this time was on a very small scale and often in illicit stills. There were, however, a few larger distilleries such as that owned by Duncan Forbes of Culloden. After his Ferintosh estates were sacked by the Jacobites in 1689, he and his descendants were granted the privilege of distilling whisky free of duty. This they did profitably until about a hundred years later. An excellent account of the rather complicated history of distilling, and the effects of excise, is given in Moss and Hume's book *The Making of Scotch Whisky* (1981).

The distilling process, which simply consists of driving off the flavoured alcohol by heat and subsequently condensing the vapour, does much to reduce its toxicity. The apparatus needed for the making of small quantities was not large and was easily concealed, which made illicit stills easy to hide. Whisky distilling was not really controlled till the Highlands of Scotland were 'subdued' after the rebellion of Prince Charles in 1745. Appropriate legislation and taxation were introduced in 1823 and led to the almost total disappearance of the illicit stills which had been so prevalent. The development of the industry during the nineteenth and twentieth centuries, in relation to distilleries and the whisky trade in general, will unfold in subsequent chapters.

In Scotland, whisky has long been, and still is, the drink of the occasion. It was used to celebrate births and marriages, and at funerals the chief mourner had a duty to regale those who attended. There was commonly an inn near the cemetery gate.

Until the middle of the nineteenth century the whisky drunk in England was the milder Lowland variety, and that in small quantity, but the whole outlook changed with the invention of the patent still in 1830 and the introduction of blending a little later. Blended whisky was popularised in London mainly by five great companies: John Dewar, James Buchanan (Black and White), James Mackie (White Horse), John Walker and John Haig, who had already established themselves in Scotland. These men deserve great credit for they not only produced whisky on which their customers could rely, but they established markets and distribution networks which brought their product first to England and then overseas. Their blends became increasingly popular: they were not so fiery or so heavy as the old Highland malts. Modern malts are, however, better made, being smoother and not so heavy.

DRINKING HABITS

Wine and brandy had been the drinks of the well-to-do in early Victorian England. However, after European vineyards had been severely affected by the phylloxera epidemic between 1858 and 1863, whisky came to take the place of brandy and was drunk by an increasing number of people. Usually it was taken by men after dinner with soda; but at this time, it was not considered to be a drink for respectable women.

After the end of Prohibition in the United States (which lasted from 1919 to 1933) cocktails became popular as an aperitif before lunch or dinner. Gin was often the basic ingredient, mixed with a variety of liqueurs or vermouth. Whisky was also used as 'whisky sour' (with lemon), or 'old-fashioned' (with angostura bitters, soda and fruit).

In 1945 Winston Churchill minuted for the Ministry of Food: 'On no account reduce the amount of barley for whisky. It takes years to mature and is an invaluable export and dollar earner. Having regard to our difficulties about export, it would be improvident not to preserve this characteristic element of British ascendancy.' During the Second World War the distilleries had done good work by making yeast for bread, alcohol to replace petrol, and acetone used in the manufacture of explosives, but cereals became in such short supply that many distilleries had to close down.

Whisky was drunk widely in English-speaking countries long before the Second World War, following which it became a fashionable drink throughout the world. It can be taken with water or soda, neat or 'on the rocks' (poured on to ice – the usual way in North America). Consumption rose in the 1960s and 1970s but fell during the recent recession. There is an obvious economic reason for this but another factor was the increasing popularity of white spirits (gin and vodka) and chilled white wine in recent years. Vigorous and attractive advertising by the Scotch Whisky industry is aimed at counteracting this and improving the image of their product.

SCOTCH TODAY

So we come to 'Scotch today'. Everything which comes from Scotland is Scottish but its whisky is 'Scotch'. Ask for a large Scotch and you get whisky.

Scotch whisky today has become a consistent product, made under very careful and skilled supervision with the best possible ingredients. Three varieties are recognised – malt whisky, grain whisky and blended whisky.

Malt whisky (chapter 2) is made entirely from a watery extract of malted barley, fermented by yeast and distilled in onion-shaped pot stills from which the flavoured alcohol is driven off by heat. Malt whisky takes from eight to fifteen years to mature but, alas, may be sold after three years. There were 117 working malt distilleries in the 1970s, but after closures in recent years there are now about 80. Nearly all the malt whisky produced is used for blending (see below), but there are now between 90 and 100 bottled single malts available. The numbers are not consistent because bottled malts, which were made some years ago, are still available although the distilleries may now be closed. It is important to appreciate that single bottled malts form a very small part of the total amount of whisky which is marketed (perhaps about 2 per cent), but the popularity of single malts is increasing and they are much more readily available now than they were in the 1970s. A vatted malt (chapter 5), as opposed to a single malt, is a whisky made of several different malts, but without a basis of grain whisky.

Grain whisky (chapter 7) is made mostly from maize, almost entirely imported, the starch of the mashed maize being broken down to maltose by adding a small quantity of malted barley. It is fermented by yeast, but it is distilled in a Coffey or patent still in which the alcohol is driven off by steam. This is a purer whisky than malt in the sense that it is nearer pure alcohol, but it has therefore appreciably less flavour and does not take so long to mature. It is also cheaper to make, but this is masked by taxation which is based on its alcoholic content. There are fewer than 10 grain distilleries now operating in Scotland, and they are all, with the exception of Invergordon, in the southern part of the country, mostly close to ports and railway lines. This makes for efficient reception of imported maize and distribution of bulk grain whisky and also because virtually all the blending and bottling establishments are in central Scotland.

The amount of grain whisky warehoused and exported in 1984 was almost 154 million litres of pure alcohol (lpa) compared with 99 million lpa of malt whisky. Grain whisky is rarely bottled on its own, but there is one exception which will be discussed later (see p.83).

Blended whisky (chapter 9) is a mixture of malt and grain whiskies, in the best blends in almost equal parts – thus securing the purity of the grain with the flavour of the malt. This is the whisky most generally available, but its quality depends on the malts it contains. There is an enormous variety of blends and Derek Cooper (1983) suggests that there are over 2000 brands of Scotch produced for sale in the home market and even more for overseas. On the other hand, it is probably true to say that there are not more than a few hundred sold in a really significant volume. Over 43 million lpa of blended whisky were produced in 1983 for domestic consumption. There are a number of de luxe blends whose superiority is related to the amount and quality of the malts used in them. Alas, many blends, some with fancy names and in fancy bottles, contain a very high proportion of grain whisky.

THE LABEL

There are now so many different kinds of whisky, that it is important for the drinker of it to be able to 'read' the label. First, make sure that the whisky is made in Scotland. This may seem obvious, but in some countries, other than Scotland, the bottle may have a name, but little else, which is related to Scotland. Many fanciful names have been attached to various blends which certainly give no indication of the quality of the whisky. Descriptive adjectives do not necessarily mean much, and there is no reason why a marginal producer's de luxe whisky is necessarily superior to a first-class standard blend. There are, however, some de luxe whiskies which contain a greater proportion of distinguished malts and which are especially delectable: they are more expensive to make and to buy. The distiller's name is obviously important, particularly to those who are reasonably well informed and this book will provide guidance in this respect.

The numbers on the label should be studied with some care. The *size* of a standard bottle is 75 cl (26⅔ fl oz) but cheaper whisky is sometimes in a 70 cl bottle. This bottle size (70 cl) is sometimes used for high-class whisky exported to the European Economic Community. There are, however, proposals to phase it out in favour of the 75 cl bottle, in order to remove the chance of the consumer being confused and reduce unfair competition in markets where both are sold. The 1 litre bottle is now becoming popular, and in duty-free shops the imperial quart (1.36 litres) is often available: a pocket calculator may be needed if value for money is to be determined.

It is important to identify the *strength* of the whisky. This has to be on the label and may give rise to some confusion. The strength of a standard blend (or malt) is expressed as 40% alcohol by volume which is the equivalent of 70° proof. The new numerical system was introduced in 1980 by the International Organisation of Legal Metrology (known by its French initials OIML). This is simpler than the older method which used 'degrees proof'. A stronger whisky at 57% alcohol by volume, for example, is the same as 100° proof. The United States has a different scale, which can lead to confusion. It is sufficient to remember that 40% alcohol by volume is the same as 70° British proof and 80° American proof. Whisky does not gain in strength as it crosses the Atlantic. Throughout this book the OIML values will be used rather than the proof and, for convenience, percentage alcohol by volume will be abbreviated to '% vol'. When the strength of an individual whisky is not recorded, it can be assumed to be 40% vol. To convert proof to OIML, should it be necessary, multiply by 4 and divide the product by 7.

The *age* of the whisky should be on the label of a malt, or better still, the year it was distilled. Generally speaking, the older the whisky, the better it is to drink, but individual malts have their own 'peak' age, perhaps between 8–15 years, after which improvement may well no longer occur. The age is usually not given on a blend, but if it is, it must represent the age of the youngest malt. This also applies to vatted malts. Single malts are all over 8 years old, and the older they are, the more expensive they are.

Finally, some labels may not be quite what they seem at first sight. Probably most drinkers, even if not quite sober, would be aware that a bottle with a label in Spanish which was headed 'Duke of Scotland' would be unlikely to contain Scotch whisky. Similar doubts might arise over Gold Castle Finest Quality Whisky disttilled (*sic*) by Theo. Vassilikis. Both these examples resulted in successful legal proceedings taken by the Scotch Whisky Association in recent years. Another more fraudulent label was illustrated in *The Times* of 16 May 1985. Two bottles were shown side by side and, even accepting that it was a monochrome newspaper photograph, the labels had similar designs and appeared the same. A second look made it clear that one was Johnnie Halker (not Walker), so in a darkened bar in a foreign country, it is just as well to observe carefully what you are drinking.

WHISKY WORLDWIDE

This book is concerned only with Scotch whisky which is made and bottled in Scotland. The precise definition of whisky is a technical and legal matter which will be considered in some detail later (chapter 7). Suffice it to say, at present, that whisky can be made outside Scotland; but when it is, the spelling of whisk*ey* is often used. Scotch whisky is here considered to be correct, even though a Royal Commission in 1909 used whiskey for both Scotch and Irish.

Irish whiskey tastes quite different and is made by a slightly different method: a wider range of cereals is used and three distillations, rather than the usual two in Scotland, are carried out. The industry is now centred near Cork where the best known Irish whiskies (Powers, Jamesons and Paddy) are produced, and very good they can be too, although not quite comparable to Scotch.

Scottish immigrants naturally introduced whisky drinking and its manufacture to North America. Corn and rye are used and Canadian whisky is referred to as rye. The taste is distinctive and little is drunk in England. American bourbon is a pleasant drink, but some Scotsmen feel that it has more after-effects than Scotch. But perhaps it depends on what you are used to.

In many other countries, local whiskey can be bought. It is usually made of indigenous spirit and perhaps some imported Scotch, and does little to deserve the name of whisky, or even whiskey. You drink it at your own risk: it is likely to produce a hangover, or worse.

A special word must be said about Japan, where more whisky is drunk than in any country except the United States. They make it too, but they often add Scotch malts (of which they import a great deal in bulk) to their own brands. The most expensive grades will contain a higher proportion of Scotch whisky and better-quality malts. De luxe Scotch whisky nonetheless remains a prestigious gift for businessmen in Japan. The Japanese have also taken up golf and Suntory, their largest whisky producers, sponsor the World Matchplay Tournament at Wentworth near London.

To return to Scotch and Scotland – perhaps with relief. The earlier editions of this book began by describing single malt whiskies: what they are like to drink and where they are made. This seems a good start but later we shall come to the blends and their makers. The aim is to introduce the reader to the many different varieties of Scotch and, while not wanting to make it too difficult, to advise a visit to some distilleries (chapter 6) where the correct pronunciation may be learnt and the whisky tasted. Finally we shall come to the way Scotch is made and the more sobering aspects of its control and marketing.

Scotland: showing the main distilleries
For details of area in dotted square see p.25.

2

Malt Whisky

A fine pot still whisky is as noble a product of Scotland as any burgundy or champagne is of France.

NEIL M. GUNN, *Whisky and Scotland*, 1935

For the most part the malt whiskies come from the Highlands of Scotland, north of Perth, country of hills and valleys, of lochs and mountain streams, of much poor land but of very good water. The barley from which they are made came originally from the coastal strips which surround the central Highlands and from a few of the beautiful valleys, but now much is imported from Lothian, Lincolnshire and East Anglia.

One river is specially associated with whisky making, the River Spey, which gives its name to the elegant Highland dance, the Strathspey. If you arrive from the south you will probably first notice the river as a small stream just as it leaves its remote mountain origins between the Caledonian Canal and the road to Inverness between Dalnaspidal and Newtonmore. It winds its way northwards, first through bare hills, then through picturesque valleys and woodlands until it reaches the rich northern plain to open into the Moray Firth at Speymouth some 10 miles north-east of Elgin. A good road accompanies it and we pass such holiday resorts as Kingussie, Aviemore and then arrive at Grantown-on-Spey where it is best to cross to the east bank of the river.

The Spey is famous for its salmon and for being the fastest-flowing river in Britain, but most of all it is famous for its whisky. There are more distilleries along the valley of the Spey and its tributaries than anywhere else in the world. Well may we ask why this is so. First and foremost the area immediately north of the Grampians has a good rainfall, peat is easily available and the coastal plain is extremely rich and suitable for growing barley. Today barley, richer in starch, is commonly brought in from the south of Scotland and England and much peat comes from Aberdeenshire. In addition – and this was very important before the days of good roads and motor cars – the region of the Spey was conveniently removed from the excisemen and illicit stills abounded. Men knew from birth how to make whisky; as the Duke of Gordon told the House of Lords, in 1822, the Highlanders were born distillers.

It has to be admitted that very few of the distilleries actually draw their water supply from the Spey itself: they get it mainly from nearby springs and wells. The river does, however, receive effluent (now carefully treated) from the distilleries and has been unkindly said to be their main drain.

At Craigellachie we can recross the Spey and, leaving it on the right, proceed by the main road north to Rothes, passing a whole series of distilleries till we reach Elgin. With the exception of the famous Glen Grant Distilleries at Rothes, the distilleries are all relatively small and similar, making excellent whisky, most of which goes to the blenders.

Elgin is, indeed, a charming county town of great character with the remains of what must have been a very beautiful cathedral, built in the thirteenth century, standing in extensive well-kept precincts adjoining a large public park. The cathedral was destroyed as long ago as 1390, by the notorious Wolf of Badenoch, Earl of Buchan, a son of King Robert II, to avenge his excommunication by the local Bishop of Moray. The king did, however, make his son do penance at the Cross which is still to be seen in the High Street.

Elgin may be described as the whisky capital of Scotland. All roads to and from it abound with distilleries and the whole of the surrounding area has rich fields of barley. In the town, too, is the imposing headquarters of Scottish Malt Distillers, which controls malt whisky production for the Distillers Company. Elgin is a centre for the bottling of the Spey whiskies, notably by Gordon & MacPhail.

As the maps show, the area around the river Spey includes most of the malt distilleries in Scotland, although there are a few on the coastal fringe to the east and north as far as Wick. Then in the west there are eight distilleries on the island of Islay, one on the island of Jura, one on Skye, two at Campbeltown, one on Mull, one at Oban and two at Fort William.

Malt whisky is, as has been said, the original whisky and is wholly distilled from fermented extract of malted barley and matured in oak casks, preferably those which have been recently used for the import of sherry. The actual process is given in more detail in chapter 8. This all sounds simple and theoretically could be done in any country, yet after hundreds of years of whisky making only the distilleries of Scotland and Ireland have survived.

We have already seen that most malt whisky is produced to make up the numerous blends which nowadays are on the market. Although it has to be recognised that this is the fate of most malt whisky, the single malt (also called the pot still malt) is a most delectable form of whisky to drink: more is available than a few years ago and more is being drunk. In previous editions of this book it was often necessary to comment 'this excellent malt can be difficult to obtain'. Fortunately this is now very much less often the case. Most supermarkets throughout the United Kingdom stock a few malts and many wine and spirit merchants stock a large number, most notably Milroy's Soho Wine Market, 3 Greek Street, London W1. Many hotels and bars and pubs stock a variable number of malts, often in surprising places. Of course, Scottish bars have always been well supplied. The following chapters describe a number of malt whiskies which we have found most agreeable to drink. Clearly the list cannot be exclusive, and if any particularly fine examples are omitted, it is because there is a limit to the number of malts any two people can sample. We should be pleased if any reader could direct us to delights which we have missed. The malts will be described in relation to the individual distilleries which they come from and it is necessary to consider them in some reasonably logical order. Geographical location is the best method and for many years the division into four groups has been accepted by the whisky trade. These are:

Highland
Islay
Campbeltown
Lowland

The Highlands are defined as that part of Scotland which lies to the north of a line drawn from Greenock (just north of Glasgow) to Dundee, and this large area produces much more whisky than the rest put together so it has to be at the top of the list. We shall discuss later distilleries which have been closed or moth-balled, but changing economic circumstances make it difficult to take accurate count. Certainly some years ago it could have been said that there were just under 120 malt distilleries and just under 100 were in the Highlands. It seems reasonable, therefore, to divide up the Highland whiskies in some way and the following is a convenient scheme:

Speyside: in the Grampian region
Northern: mostly on the east coast north of Inverness
Eastern: on the east coast, north and south of Aberdeen
Perthshire: now in the Tayside region
Island: this is a mixed bag of distilleries on Orkney, Skye, Jura and Mull (remember Islay whiskies are a separate group because of their special characteristics).

The maps on pages 15 and 25 indicate the sites of the various distilleries which will be described. The aim is to give some indication of the whereabouts of the distillery, its history and the quality of its products. The name given at the head of each section is the name of a single malt rather than the distillery. This seems a pedantic point, and names change in time, but the inquiring reader may notice what might appear to be a discrepancy in the text. The amount of detail will vary, depending on our experience.

Although we are now about to discuss single malts and the distilleries which make them, it is important to emphasise that almost all their whisky goes for blending and this is the main contribution which they make to the Scotch whisky industry as a whole.

The history of many distilleries often has a familiar pattern which follows this general outline: establishment more than a hundred yeas ago, commonly on the site of a much older illicit still used by smugglers and close to a source of suitable and abundant water. In the later part of the nineteenth century there was a boom in whisky production and it was at this time most distilleries were visited by Alfred Barnard. His book, *The Whisky Distilleries of the United Kingdom*, is not only a delight to read but is a key source of historical information. After Barnard, the success story continued until the First World War (1914–1918) when production was reduced and then stopped. Some distilleries recovered, but only for a short time, since Prohibition in the USA and the depression of the 1920s took their toll of the whisky trade. Not only were there closures, but plant and machinery was taken out. Some revived in the 1930s, only to fail again when whisky making was curtailed by strict rationing of cereals in the Second World War (1939–1945).

As prosperity returned to the United Kingdom in the late 1960s, there was a dramatic increase in demand for whisky. The export market is extremely important and in the postwar period 80–85 per cent of all Scotch whisky (blends and malts) was exported compared with 50 per cent in 1938–9. Distilleries were reopened, enlarged and rebuilt. The consumer was encouraged to take an interest and some excellent reception centres were opened. Competition led to vigorous advertising (but not on television) and business flourished. There were many takeovers and mergers by large organisations, national and international, but in most cases the name of the original owners continued to be used. Some independent and privately owned companies survived and prospered, but they were the exception.

An indication of the expansion can be seen in a list of the distilleries, and their parent companies, which were built on Speyside during the 1960s and 1970s:

1960	Tormore	Long John International
1965	Tomintoul	Whyte & Mackay
1966	Tamnavulin	Invergordon Distillers
1968	Glenallachie	Waverley
1974	Pittyvaich	Bell's
1974	Braes of Glenlivet	Seagram
1975	Allt à Bhainne	Seagram

This building programme reflects the increasing demand for blended whisky 10 or 20 years ago, but the most recent distilleries have hardly been working long enough to produce a mature malt. Two other new distilleries are Loch Lomond built in 1966 (Amalgamated Distilled Products) and Auchroisk in 1974 (International Distillers and Vintners). These were the years when the prosperity of the whisky industry seemed assured. Another facet was the involvement of Canadian investment and this can be seen by the number of important Speyside malt distillers acquired or built by Seagram:

The Glenlivet	Strathisla
Glen Grant	Glen Keith
Longmorn	Allt à Bhainne
Benriach	Braes of Glenlivet

Scotch whisky undoubtedly enlarged its franchise immensely in the world-wide consumer boom which began in the 1950s and so suffered correspondingly after the energy crisis, beginning in 1973, had reduced the consumers' spending power. As a consequence a number of distilleries have had to close in the 1980s. This has always happened when the market has become overstocked, as is the case today. An abbreviated quotation from Moss & Hume (1981) is apposite: 'Between 1824 and 1857 . . . the problem of over-capacity and over-production . . . remained unresolved. Many of the small rural distilleries . . . had been forced to close down. . . . The industry's problems had been increased by the growth of the temperance movement and anti-spirits campaign . . . and led to a further decline in consumption.' Thus history repeats itself.

The cyclical pattern will be evident in the history of many of the distilleries which will now be described. Since the story is one of troughs and peaks, it is to be hoped, and surely expected, that better times will come and we shall see closed distilleries opening again and producing good malt whisky. The only thing that fortunately does not change is the splendid scenery in the more remote parts of Scotland where many of the distilleries are situated.

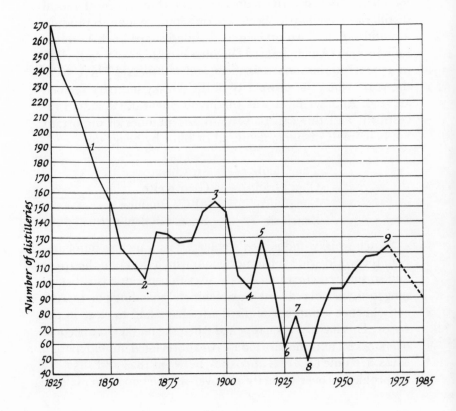

The graph on the opposite page shows the number of working distilleries in Scotland given as an average in each five-year period from 1825 to 1985 (the numbers are listed in Moss and Hume's *The Making of Scotch Whisky*). The vertical axis gives the numbers of distilleries and the horizontal axis each five-year period.

1 The decline in the number of distilleries was accompanied by a rise in the production of whisky: the smaller distilleries were closing and larger ones were opening.
2 Slump due to Sprits Act of 1860 which increased duty.
3 Rise due to increased sales of blended whisky.
4 Slump following overproduction in the 1890s and the First World War.
5 Post First World War boom.
6 Depression of the late 1920s and early 1930s (and Prohibition).
7 Temporary recovery.
8 Severe decline during the Second World War.
9 Recovery after the Second World War with increasing prosperity in the 1960s and 1970s.
10 Probable decline after recession in the late 1970s.

NB: Although the graph reflects the trends by recording the average number of working distilleries in each quinquenium, this does not parallel the amount of whisky produced. For example, in 1910, 124 distilleries produced about 22 million proof gallons of whisky, whereas in 1935, 64 distilleries produced nearly 17 million proof gallons.

3

The Highland Malts

*The Highlands are the home of
malt whisky and always will be. . . .
Here nature has been generous in her gifts.*
ROBERT BRUCE LOCKHART, *Scotch,* 1967

SPEYSIDE MALTS

The country around the river Spey is the heartland of Scotch malt whisky, but the map will show that some of the distilleries are in what might be regarded as far flung outposts of this particular empire. No classification is perfect and the malts included here are generally regarded as Speyside malts. To subdivide them by separating the Glenlivets is, as will be clear, both artificial and meaningless.

First, seven malts will be described which are made in what may be regarded as truly Speyside distilleries. The remainder are related to the nearest towns or villages: Rothes; Elgin; Dufftown; Keith and, finally, three outliers which are situated towards the north-east and the sea.

THE GLENLIVET

> *Glenlivet has its castles three,*
> *Dromin, Blairfindy and Deskie,*
> *And also one distillery*
> *More famous than the castles three.*

No excuse is needed for giving this whisky pride of place

amongst the malts, for The Glenlivet has been the prince of whiskies for over a hundred years. In 1880 under threat of legal proceedings an agreement was reached by which it became the only whisky entitled to call itself The Glenlivet as it was the only whisky made in the parish of Glenlivet, but certain other whiskies were permitted to use the name provided it was prefixed by another name. No fewer than 23 availed themselves of

This map shows the main towns and distilleries in the Speyside area. Most are described in Chapter 3, but others included are mentioned elsewhere in the book.

the honour and Glenlivet has been called sarcastically the longest glen in Scotland. Some distilleries which use the suffix '– Glenlivet' are 20 miles distant and at least one hasn't even a distillery. Nowadays the better-known malts, such as The Macallan, Strathisla and Longmorn, amongst others, no longer use the suffix Glenlivet.

The Livet is a small tributary of the river Avon which enters the Spey half-way between Grantown-on-Spey and Craigellachie and collects water from the northern foothills of the Grampians. Before the days of the local railway and the motor car, this was indeed a remote area – a high barley-bearing plateau and not too far from the rich northern plain with good water and peat. It was ideally suited for illicit whisky making and in 1820 there were said to be 200 illicit stills in the area.

The old Glenlivet distillery was at Drumin, a farm further up the hill than the present one. It was burnt down in 1858. The new distillery is in a commanding position, like the old castles in its view.

The Glenlivet distillery was the first to be licensed, when the Government in 1823, on the recommendation of the Duke of Richmond and Gordon, made an offer to license small distilleries cheaply. Prior to that, by a law of 1814, stills of under 500 gallons were illegal but that statute was generally ignored. In licensing his distillery the owner George Smith took a personal risk for he was considered by his neighbours to be a 'black leg'. He was, however, a robust Scot of the best type who was always prepared to defend his rights and especially his property. He also had the support of the local landowners who were anxious to 'clean up' the glen. Indeed one, the Laird of Aberlour, presented George Smith with a pair of pistols with which to defend himself. About this time one distillery on Deeside was actually burnt down by the objectors to regulation. It was several years before the trouble died down. The Smith family were also prominent as farmers and in the conduct of local affairs. Their history is well given in The Glenlivet centenary volume published in 1924 (reprinted in 1964) and in Robert Bruce Lockhart's book (1959).

There are also many stories about The Glenlivet whisky. David Daiches in *Scotch Whisky* (1983) refers to King George IV's visit to Scotland in 1822 and quotes Elizabeth Grant of Rothiemurchus that 'the King drank nothing else but Glenlivet whisky'. He also recalls that earlier the King, on his arrival at Leith, had, in J. G. Lockhart's words, 'called for a bottle of Highland whisky, and desired a glass to be filled' – for Sir Walter Scott. 'Sir Walter, after draining his own bumper, made the request that the King would condescend to bestow on him the glass out of which his Majesty had just drunk his health.' Daiches continues: 'This is the glass that Scott, having put it in his pocket, forgot about when, on arriving home, he found the poet Crabbe awaiting him. He sat down on it and smashed it to pieces giving him a painful, but insignificant scratch.' Daiches finally comments that there is no record of whether the Highland whisky consumed on that occasion was Glenlivet or not. But it seems quite likely that it was, in view of the King's known partiality for this particular whisky.

The Smith family continued to own the distillery until 1978, when Seagram bought The Glenlivet and Glen Grant distilleries.

The Glenlivet whisky has a deep mellowness and ripe fullness of flavour together with a delicacy of aroma which is easy to recognise. It has a subtle peatiness without being aggressively peaty and a gentle sweetness without any loss of freshness. The distillery has the single malt bottled at 12 years and 40% vol. It carries with it the tradition of the glen and its pioneer distillers. It now has the distinction of being the largest selling malt in the US.

The distillery does not use Livet water but draws supplies from local wells where peat and granite are not conspicuous. Its peat continues to be cut at Faemussach Moss nearby and its barley comes from the Laich of Moray and neighbouring farms.

There is, opposite The Glenlivet distillery, a Dark Grains Plant which processes draff (p.89) and pot ale (p.92) from a number of distilleries. It uses modern techniques and employs very little labour.

THE MACALLAN

Here we have a whisky of quality; indeed, many consider it to be the best. It has a smooth richness of flavour quite its own. The distillery, like so many, had its origin on a farm. Macallan's farm is in the ancient Macallan parish on the hill just above the ford at Craigellachie near where the Telford bridge, built in 1814, now stands. The small old parish churchyard is within the distillery property. Here, in the late eighteenth century, cattle from the Moray coastal plain were assembled before crossing the river to the long drove road through the mountain passes to Falkirk and the other southern markets. It is easy to understand how the herdsmen spread the fame of this delicious whisky.

The distillery was one of the first (1824) to accept the Government offer to license distilleries for a small fee. In due course it passed into the hands of Alexander Reid, who had it until 1886 when it was sold to James Stuart. The latter sold it in 1892 to Roderick Kemp, who added to the buildings considerably. Kemp died in 1909 and the distillery was run by a trust for the family until 1946, when the private limited company Macallan-Glenlivet Ltd was formed.

Macallan-Glenlivet PLC became a public company in 1964 and now has a market capitalisation of £15 million. Robert Kemp's descendants have retained large shareholdings, so that there is still close family control of the company.

By 1966 a second distillery was built alongside the first to meet increasing demands. There were difficult times in the 1970s, but much more of the single bottled malt has been available for sale since 1980. In recent years profits have increased significantly. Their main export market is Italy.

The Macallan has always maintained a high quality and is generally accepted as being one of the best three Highland malts. It is now available at various ages: for example, 10 years old in two strengths (40% and 57% vol which corresponds to 70° proof and 100° proof) and 25 years old at 40% vol. The whisky is always matured in sherry casks, and they have gone as far as deciding by experiment that an oloroso cask is the best type to use. The suffix – Glenlivet – has now been dropped from the name on the label, which is surely a sign of confidence. I know of no better malt than Macallan 1952 or 1953. These are, unfortunately, no longer available but we still have carefully preserved a few bottles remaining from a case bought about twenty years ago. It is delicious and showing no sign of deterioration. Like all malts, the quality can vary from year to year and there is no explanation for this. The story of Sir James Howie and the 1954 Macallan has been told in the Preface.

To celebrate the royal marriage in 1981, a special Wedding Malt was produced. Malts distilled during 1948 and 1961, which are the years when the Prince of Wales and Lady Diana Spencer were born, were vatted together – a nice touch.

CARDHU

This single malt was reintroduced in 1965, although a whisky spelled Cardow, but pronounced Cardhu, from the distillery had been available earlier. When I first tasted it, I was not impressed. It seemed just another malt. Perhaps the expensive new advertisements had made me expect too much. Later, however, when I took it after a blend and with haggis it was much more worthy. This emphasises the point that a whisky may taste quite differently according to its accompaniments and the circumstances in which it is taken. Cardhu is a good Speyside whisky which has never claimed to be a Glenlivet.

Distilling appears to have been going on in this remote area from quite early times but the first legal distillery at Cardow was founded there by John Cumming in 1824. Its whisky soon acquired a good reputation and was taken by horse and cart to the little port of Burghead on the north coast of Moray and thence shipped to Leith.

The distillery has a striking situation at Knockando overlooking the Spey valley, and its beautifully kept stillhouse, with six great shining copper stills in a row, is a really magnificent sight.

It was bought from the Cumming family in 1893 by John Walker of Kilmarnock and its whisky no doubt became part of the famous Johnnie Walker blends.

Cardow was transferred to SMD in 1930 under the umbrella of Distillers. There is sometimes confusion between the spelling of Cardow and Cardhu, the latter being Gaelic. The place is Cardow and the malt is Cardhu, but in 1984 the distillery was renamed Cardhu, so now presumably we can forget about the other spelling. A 12-years-old malt is available which is characterised by its sweetish taste. The bottle is shaped like a decanter with hollow sides and is corked (rather than having a screw cap).

A visitors' centre is being planned with enthusiasm and with the hope that the distillery will be part of the Whisky Trail.

TAMDHU

The Tamdhu Distillery Company was founded in 1897. It was subscribed to by a number of well-known distillers, but they rapidly sold out and the Company operated only for a year. It was then taken over by Highland Distilleries who have owned it ever since. The depression forced closure in 1927 and the distillery was not reopened till 1948 when there was a renewed demand for whisky after the war. Extensive rebuilding was undertaken during the mid-1970s. The old railway station of Knockando, within a few hundred yards of the main buildings, makes a small, but most attractive, reception area and shop. Malting is carried out in Saladin boxes and the arrangements for seeing the rest of the distillery are exceptional since a large gallery surrounds the working area. Spectators are kept away from the 'machinery', but have a remarkably good view of it.

The whisky is a typical Glenlivet with a good flavour and is not too peaty. It is bottled by the proprietors at 10 years 40% vol and 15 years 43% vol.

KNOCKANDO

The Knockando distillery was built by Ian Thompson in 1898 and although situated in a lonely area, the Cardhu and Tamdhu distilleries are nearby. The land below the property slopes abruptly down to the swirling waters of the Spey. All workmen live in tied cottages which cluster around the distillery. There has been debate about the precise meaning of Cnoc-an-dhu, but experts in Gaelic consulted by Justerini & Brooks confirm that 'little black hillock' is correct. The water is drawn from the Cardnach Spring.

There is no evidence to show that Thompson worked the distillery after 1902 when overproduction was probably responsible for the collapse of the market. W. & A. Gilbey bought the distillery in 1904 for the exceptionally modest price of £3500. In 1962 Gilbey amalgamated with Justerini & Brooks and others to form the International Distillers & Vintners Ltd.

The distillery was rebuilt in 1969 and has an annual capacity of 500,000 gallons. The single malt is bottled by Justerini & Brooks at 12 years old and there is also an 'extra old' which has been distilled 21 or more years previously. The elegant label is unusually informative as it gives both the year of distilling ('the Season') and the year of bottling, as well as the strength which is 43% vol (75° proof). The time of bottling is carefully chosen for each cask when the whisky is judged to be at its best. It is agreeable to drink, and is surprisingly light for a Speyside malt, but nevertheless it is mellow with a distinctive finish.

TORMORE

Tormore, which is near the village of Advie, was the first new Highland distillery to be built this century. The company which took this initiative in 1958 was Seager Evans, who changed their name to Long John International in 1971. The architect was Professor Sir Albert Richardson, past President of the Royal Academy, and his building fits well into its Scottish surroundings. There is an elegant lantern over the cooperage with a clock that chimes and plays 'Highland Laddie' several times at the hour. The water comes from the Advockie Burn which runs down from near Loch-an-Oir (which means Loch of Gold).

The single malt has a really rich flavour without being noticeably peaty. It is bottled at the distillery at 10 years old and 40% vol. It is a whisky with its own appeal and to this is added the design of the new bottle which might be described as 'fancy' but fits the hand well.

GLENFARCLAS

The distillery was begun in 1836 by Robert Hay and probably developed from a farm on the rich lands below the great hills which were the home of golden eagle, ptarmigan, wild cat and red deer. Glenfarclas means 'glen of the green grasslands'. The site is somewhat isolated, near Ballindalloch where the River Avon joins the Spey.

John Grant bought the tenancy, and with it the distillery, in 1865. He farmed and for five years leased the distillery to John Smith, who was a brewer from Glenlivet. In 1870 Smith left to set up his own distillery at Cragganmore and the Grants took up distilling themselves. This is truly a family concern and remains independent of other large companies, although it might be surmised that tempting offers of purchase have been resisted. John Grant is the managing director, although his father, George Grant, continues to take a very active interest in the business as chairman.

There have been many improvements in recent years and everything is beautifully kept. In the mash house there are delightful murals by the painter Edward Halliday. The stills themselves are unusually large and are heated by gas. The reception centre has an excellent exhibition and a dining room which is lined with panelling from the *Empress of Australia*. About 60,000 visitors are received each year.

The water is drawn from the Green Burn which rises in Ben Rinnes, the hill behind the distillery. Malted barley is now bought in from Kirkcaldy and elsewhere.

The whisky is a fine full-flavoured malt so popular with the blenders that most of it is sold before it is made. The single malt is now available at varying ages from 8 to 25 years and from 40% vol to 60% vol. It is bottled for the proprietors and sold in the UK through Saccone & Speed. The quality remains consistently high and there is no 'topping up' during the period of maturation. An advertisement proclaims: 'Of all the whiskies, malt is the King. Of all the Kings, Glenfarclas reigns supreme'.

But to return to practicalities: there is a plant half a mile from the distillery which processes the by-products from Glenfarclas, and from neighbouring distilleries, converting them into cattle feed.

ABERLOUR-GLENLIVET

The distillery is on the main road to the south of the town of Aberlour, where it is tucked into a steep little valley which the river Lour has carved out on its way to the Spey. Its water comes from the slopes of Ben Rinnes, which dominates the surrounding countryside, and supplies water to many nearby distilleries. In the distillery grounds is the Well of St Drostan, an Englishman and patron saint of Aberlour, who was a missionary in these parts before becoming Archbishop of Canterbury in 959. He was later canonised as St Dunstan. Originally there were mills in the valley, but there has been a distillery here since 1826. It was rebuilt in 1879 after a fire, and had several owners, amongst whom was Holt of Manchester who bought it in 1920 and produced Holt's Mountain Cream. Holt sold it in 1945 to S. Campbell & Sons. It is one of the tidiest and best-kept distilleries I know.

In 1974 the House of Campbell was taken over by the Pernod Ricard Group, thus establishing a French interest in the Scotch whisky industry.

The whisky is smooth, round and has a distinctive flavour which is said to owe its characteristics to the use of barley which is 'not fat, but with high protein' and its water made famous by

St Drostan ten centuries ago. It is now bottled at 12 years and 40% vol.

GLENROTHES

Rothes is another of the great distillery centres and when Barnard (1887) visited the town, three distilleries were operating and producing 350,000 gallons a year, while almost a million gallons were stored in bonded warehouses.

Glenrothes distillery lies to the east up the Burn of Rothes and has a good supply of water from the Mannoch Hills. It was built in 1878 and the original proprietors were W. Grant & Son. Ten years later Glenrothes was bought by the Islay Distillery Company, and Highland Distilleries Ltd was formed. Additional stills were added in 1980 making 10 altogether.

The single malt is a delicious whisky which is deservedly popular. It is mostly bottled at 8 years, but more recently Gordon & MacPhail have bottled a 1954 distillation; this is described by the Harrods tasting panel (1983) as 'a touch fiery and a touch antiseptic at the very finish, but a fine old dram for a cold day'.

GLEN GRANT

Glen Grant may not be a place on the map but the fame of this whisky is sufficient to make people look for it, and the Grants of Strathspey have been making whisky legally or otherwise since distilling began. It must be remembered, too, that in these parts a very large proportion of the population bears the noble name of Grant. Castle Grant is near Grantown-on-Spey, but the distillery is in Rothes.

The Glen Grant distillery was founded by John and James Grant in 1840, but the brothers, who came from Inveravon, appear to have been distilling on the farm of Dandaleith nearby from 1834. Since its foundation there has been a process of gradual modernisation. The credit for the fame of Glen Grant is given to a George Grant who had been manager of Linkwood distillery not far away. He had made a special study of distilling and made many changes in Glen Grant distillery.

There was another distillery across the street in Rothes which had been begun by James Grant, son of the original founder, in 1898, but it was caught in the slump at the end of the century and closed down in 1902. In 1965 this was reopened after complete modernisation and a large amount of automation. It has been given the name Caperdonich after the well from which both distilleries draw water.

The firm of J. & J. Grant, Glen Grant Ltd, was formed in 1932 amalgamating in 1953 with George and J. G. Smith Ltd of The Glenlivet to form The Glenlivet and Glen Grant Distilleries Ltd. In 1970 Longmorn and Hill Thomson became subsidiaries. The company was acquired by Seagram in 1978.

Glen Grant whisky at its best has a distinction and flavour which is different from other Speysides. Before the Second World War many would have said it was the best malt and I had some without a date of smooth, almost unbelievable quality.

Single malt Glen Grants are available up to 33 years old in a variety of strengths, but I still prefer the 15 years old (40% vol). It is on the overseas market at 5 years and is now the market leader in Italy.

LONGMORN

Longmorn distillery is on the main road between Rothes and Elgin, and its malt whisky has long been recognised to be one of the best Speysides. The distillery was built in 1893–4 by John Duff and was near an old water-driven meal mill which has been known to exist since 1600. This is now used as a dwelling house.

The name is probably Welsh from 'Llanmorgund' – Morgund, or Morgan, the holy man. A warehouse now stands where the old chapel used to be. The water comes from a local spring which never dries, and the peat is obtained from the nearby Mannoch Hill.

The sons of James Grant ran the distillery after 1898, together with nearby Benriach. In 1970 Glen Grant, Longmorn and Hill Thompson merged to form The Glenlivet Distillers Ltd, which was subsequently taken over by Seagram in 1978.

The single malt, sold at 12 years old (40% vol) has an outstanding bouquet worth a brandy glass after dinner. A mixture of The Glenlivet or The Macallan, with Longmorn, and with perhaps a dash of Clynelish, makes what is probably the best drink in the world.

The lasting power of this whisky was demonstrated when David Daiches drank it from a freshly broached cask in 1967 when it was 68 years old. He described it as being pleasant and mellow, although it had lost strength and body.

GLEN ELGIN

Glen Elgin is near Longmorn, just south of Elgin. It was one of the last distilleries to be built in the speculative boom of the 1890s. The founders were William Simpson and James Carle, and production began in 1900. By this time there were economic difficulties following the Pattison crash (see p. 131) and it is said that none of the contractors or craftsmen had been paid in full except for the steeplejacks, who threatened to demolish a chimney unless they got their money. Six months after opening, the distillery was up for sale, so bad was the financial situation. It was sold in 1901 to the Glen Elgin-Glenlivet Distillery Company which was acquired by J. J. Blanche & Co Ltd, of Glasgow, in 1906. They sold the distillery to Scottish Malt Distillers Ltd in 1930.

Ability to increase the output of a particular distillery is governed by four factors: the adequacy of the water supply, the restrictions of the site, the means of disposing of the effluent and the paramount need to maintain the character of the 'make'. These conditions could be met at Glen Elgin and in 1964 considerable rebuilding was carried out and the number of stills increased from four to six.

The distiller's licence is held by White Horse Distillers Ltd, proprietors of White Horse and Logan blended Scotch whisky. They bottle Glen Elgin as a single malt at 12 years old (43% vol); it is recommended by Brian Spiller as 'a good dram'.

LINKWOOD

This charming distillery is in a wood near Elgin and was built in 1821, being named after an old mansion which was on the site. George Brown, Provost of Elgin, was the original owner and his son rebuilt the distillery in 1874. Scottish Malt Distillers bought it in 1933 and John McEwan & Co Ltd now hold the licence. Much rebuilding was carried out in 1962 and again in 1971.

The reputation of Linkwood whisky was the pride of Roderick Mackenzie, a Gaelic-speaking native of Wester Ross who for many years supervised its making 'with unremitting vigilance'. Not one item of equipment was ever replaced unless it had to be and it is said not even a spider's web could be removed. Linkwood is a pleasant light whisky with a typical Speyside flavour although it reminds me of the Lowland Rosebank. It is not well known but has long been classified as one of the best. I have known Linkwood produce a really superb whisky but, as the year was not on the bottle, I could not identify it.

It is now available at 12 years old. Gordon & MacPhail have bottled it from distillations of 1938 and 1939 although these must be becoming scarce.

DUFFTOWN-GLENLIVET

If we leave the Spey at Craigellachie and travel east, we reach the top of a hill which looks down into the unique whisky basin of Dufftown with its seven distilleries: Dufftown-Glenlivet, Balvenie, Glenfiddich, Mortlach, Glendullan, Convalmore and, the most recently built, Pittyvaich. This is a relatively remote part of Scotland: but the abundant water and peat, and at one time barley, was the reason why it became a centre for whisky-making.

During the Second World War when whisky was transported by train, the inhabitants of Dufftown would know when a consignment was leaving, because of the noise of an unusual amount of shunting, and were always ready with suitable receptacles in case a wagon leaked.

The Dufftown-Glenlivet distillery lies in the Dullan Glen, but gets its water from the Highlandman's Glen in the Conval Hills some miles away. The Dullan Water, however, provides the power and the distillery was built on the site of a mill. It was founded in 1896 by a syndicate which later became P. Mac-Kenzie & Co, Distillers, of Edinburgh. Arthur Bell & Son Ltd bought this company in 1933 which also owned the Blair Athol distillery (closed at that time because of the slump) and which had a great deal of whisky stored in warehouses in other parts of Scotland. Bell's also acquired extensive lands around Pittyvaich, close by Dufftown, where they built a new distillery in 1974. At this time they added two new stills to the old distillery, and two more in 1979. Additional warehouses have also been built.

The Dufftown-Glenlivet whisky is much sought after by blenders, but a single malt is bottled at 8 years and 14 years. The 8 years old is a typical peaty Speyside malt. It is slightly sweetish and particularly good to drink after dinner.

GLENFIDDICH

The story of William Grant of Glenfiddich is fascinating. He was born in 1839, the son of a poor soldier who served with Wellington in the Peninsular War. After leaving school in Dufftown, he was apprenticed to a shoemaker but later became the manager of a lime works. He had hoped to set up a lime works for himself, but having no capital he eventually, in 1866, entered Mortlach distillery where he worked for twenty years, during which time he not only learnt all he could about distilling and construction, but saved some money.

His chance came when he was able to buy the equipment of the old Cardow distillery for £120 and with his sons, and a little outside help, he built Glenfiddich distillery which began work in 1887. In the financing of the distillery he was assisted by his two eldest sons, one of whom had become a lawyer and the other a schoolmaster. With three of his younger sons he ran the distillery for the first two years, during which time two of these three sons prepared themselves for entrance to Aberdeen University where they eventually became doctors of medicine. The third son, after a period at sea, bought nearby Glendronach distillery (which was sold to Teacher's in 1960). The first William Grant died in 1923 at the age of eighty-three.

Glenfiddich, having had such a founder, flourished from the beginning, so much so that a second distillery – Balvenie – was built nearby. Both are on the little river Fiddich which flows into the Spey.

In 1955 Glenfiddich distillery was rebuilt to double its capacity. It now has 12 active stills which are unusually small and coal-fired. In spite of its size, the distillery employs only four men on each of three shifts. This is the only Highland distillery to bottle its own malt whisky on the spot.

An old barn has been converted into a visitors' centre with rooms for receptions and other activities; about 1000 people, many from overseas, arrive each day during the summer. Many of the buildings are attractive in themselves and William Grant's original office has been preserved.

The single malt has a good fruity taste with a peaty flavour. The triangular bottle has become familiar all over the world. The age is not on the label, but it is mostly 8 years old with the addition of a small quantity of 12 years old to each vatting, which gives depth to its flavour without impairing the characteristic freshness.

In 1963 the company decided to concentrate on promoting Glenfiddich as a single malt. A carefully planned campaign produced progressively increasing sales in the UK and overseas, culminating in the Queen's Award for Export Achievement in 1974. Glenfiddich is now the biggest-selling single malt whisky. Their campaign has undoubtedly led to a general increase in popularity of the other malts as well as their own.

BALVENIE

The ruins of Balvenie Castle in Dufftown date back to the thirteenth century. This was where the Fair Maid of Galloway wed two of the Black Douglases. The first was murdered and the second was defeated by King James II in 1455. The King is said to have been so taken with the Fair Maid's beauty that he reinstated her in Balvenie Castle for the annual rent of a single red rose. A second 'modern' castle or mansion house, designed by the Adam brothers, was built in the fields below in 1724. This, too, was abandoned and William Grant, having made a success of nearby Glenfiddich converted the ruined buildings into a distillery in 1892. It remains the only Highland distillery to farm its own barley and still has a traditional malting floor. The water from the Robbie Dubh continues to be used for mashing.

The original single malt had quite a different flavour from Glenfiddich and it is difficult to know why as the same water and barley are used for both. A theoretical explanation could be the size and method of heating the stills: the stills at Balvenie are much larger than those at Glenfiddich and are heated by steam rather than being directly over the coalfire. But the flavour of any whisky is always difficult to explain.

William Grant & Co have recently produced two new superior malts. The Founder's Reserve is made from whiskies distilled at Balvenie and matured for 8 or 9 years. Finally, there is a careful and judicious vatting from 60 or more casks to produce the desired character. The shape of the long-necked bottle is reminiscent of the Balvenie stills. Even more upmarket is the Classic, bottled in a flagon which is said to represent the doors of the old peat kiln. The strength is 43% vol, but there is no indication of the age on the label (the only date is 1892 which is when the distillery was founded). But the youngest spirit in the Classic is 12 years old and some is older. At least one year before bottling, it is transferred from oak to oloroso sherry casks which accounts for its darker colour and richness. Both these whiskies will initially have a limited distribution outside Scotland. It is hoped, and expected, that they will share the recent fame of Glenfiddich to which they are considered by William Grant to be the perfect complement.

MORTLACH

Mortlach in Dufftown has an interesting history. It was in this dell that Malcolm, the Scottish King, defeated the Danes in 1010 by damming the little river Dullan a mile upstream. The Danes, attracted by the pleasant bowl, camped in it – the word Mortlach means the bowl-shaped valley – but at night the dam was broken and the Danes were overwhelmed by the water and the Scots. As a thanksgiving for the victory Malcolm added '3 spears' length' to Mortlach Church, which had been founded in 566.

In a previous edition of this book the single malt was described as fruity and lush with more peat than it used to have. The distillery remains open but, alas, Distillers Company have decided no longer to issue the single malt. However, decreasing quantities, including a 1938 distillation, may be around for a short time – it might still be worth looking for this excellent malt.

GLENDULLAN

Another famous distillery of Dufftown, which was built in 1897 for William Williams of Aberdeen. After the First World War, this company was merged with Alexander & Macdonald of Leith and the old firm of Greenlees Brothers (1840) of London and Glasgow, under the title of Macdonald Greenlees & Williams, which joined the Distillers Company in 1926 as Macdonald Greenlees. A second distillery, also called Glendullan, was built on the site in 1971–2.

Glendullan became available as a single malt in 1972. It is

indeed a really grand whisky, robust and full of character and flavour, but mellow. Naturally it is the basis of the well-known blends of Macdonald Greenlees, but it is bottled at 12 years old, 40% vol.

STRATHISLA

This is a rich full-flavoured whisky in the best tradition of Speysides. Anyone drinking the 15 years old for the first time will remark on its excellence, which is somewhat like that of Mortlach. The malt is also bottled at 8, 12, and 30 years.

It is made at Keith, a considerable distance from the Livet. The town is the centre of the great barley-growing plain in the north of Banffshire and is of historical interest, having associations with the Duke of Montrose during the reign of Charles I. The history of whisky making in Keith goes back long before this and C. S. McBain of Chivas Brothers, who has provided me with much information, tells me that Malcolm, Vicar of Keith, and his fellow churchmen produced 'heather ale' in 1208.

In 1786 a local merchant, George Taylor, and a local factor, Alexander Milne, obtained a jack or charter from the Earl of Findlater and Seafield to build a distillery. Many conditions were imposed on them, including providing materials, along with other tenants for 'the building and repairing of the Kirk, Kirkyard dykes, minister's manse and offices and school and schoolhouse . . .' and much more. A copy of the original document stills exists and the bicentenary of this event will be celebrated on St Summarius Day, on 2 September 1986.

The distillery was initially called Milton and the mashing water was, and still is, drawn from the Broomhill spring which had been a holy well of the local Cistercian monks. It is said to be guarded by kelpies or water-sprites.

William Longmore, a local banker and merchant, took over the distillery in 1821 and set about improving and expanding it. Barnard showed sketches of Milton in his book *The Whisky Distilleries*. Although there has been a good deal of rebuilding since the late nineteenth century, the double pagoda roofs and the general appearance have an air of careless antiquity, a state encouraged by the enterprising Samuel Bronfman of Seagram, and a tradition continued by the present Bronfman family.

The distillery has seen exciting times, with a fire in 1876 and an explosion in 1879. Nonetheless, whisky production expanded to meet the increased demand in the first quarter of this century. There was an unpleasant episode after the Second World War, when a London financier bought up shares in Longmore & Co and eventually became Chairman. There was talk of the whisky being bottled under an assumed name and sold on the black market. The business deteriorated to a degree that a government inquiry was set up and the financier was found guilty of tax evasion on a large scale. His assets were confiscated and the distillery was sold in 1950 at a public auction for £71,000. The purchaser was James Barclay, managing director of Messrs Chivas Brothers, who was a very influential figure in the world of Scotch whisky. Many improvements followed and the reputation of the distillery was restored. Chivas Brothers had been purchased by Seagram in 1948 and so the Bronfman family became involved in Milton.

The whisky had always been called Strathisla. It was sold in stone jars in the early days and from 1920 in dark brown glass bottles. The name of the distillery was changed from Milton to Strathisla in 1951.

The single malt is available at ages from 8 to 35 years and at various strengths from 40% vol to 50% vol.

AULTMORE

Aultmore distillery near Keith was built by Alexander Edward of Sanquhar, Forres, during the years 1895–6, and in July 1897 distilling was started. Up to 1898 Edward was the sole proprietor but, on his acquisition of Oban distillery in that year, he floated a limited liability company called the Oban & Aultmore Glenlivet Distillery Co Ltd of which he was managing director.

In 1923 Aultmore distillery was sold to John Dewar & Sons Ltd, from whom it was transferred to Scottish Malt Distillers Ltd in October 1930 and licensed to John & Robert Harvey Co Ltd.

Many improvements were made to the distillery in the early 1970s. The 12 years old single malt is now readily available and is highly regarded.

GLENDRONACH

This distillery is near Huntly in the valley of Forgue and on the Dronach Burn from which the whisky takes it name. It was built in 1826 by James Allardyce and others and was one of the earliest distilleries in the Highlands to be licensed. After a serious fire in 1837, the ownership passed to a Walter Scott (not the author). The Glendronach malt gained a high reputation in Scotland and England. Captain Charles Grant, son of Major William Grant, became owner in 1920. Teacher's bought the distillery from the Grants in 1960.

At one time the malt had a label and blue tag 'most suitable for medicinal purposes'. This was removed by Teacher's. It is now available at 12 years old and 40% vol.

INCHGOWER

Inchgower has been available as a single malt only since 1972. The distillery, which is just inland from Buckie, was built a hundred years previously. Alexander Wilson had established a distillery at Tochineal in 1822 and the family business was moved to Inchgower in 1871. Water was drawn from the Letter Burn which runs past the distillery into the sea, and also from the water of Aultmore.

The distillery was bought by Bell's in 1936: the original owners had gone into liquidation and sold it to Buckie Town Council a few years previously. A. K. Bell paid £3000 and increased his bargain by purchasing a nearby mansion for £1000. The Provost of Buckie is reputed to have said in recent

years that 'it was the first time I was done twice in one day'.
Bell's introduced modern methods and increased production
considerably. Jack House, writing in *Pride of Perth*, recalls the
manager Ned Shaw who was obviously a great character and
had tremendous experience of whisky making. In due course
we shall come to Shaw's method of drinking which includes
'shoogling' the mixture around the mouth.

Much of the Inchgower malt must go into Bell's blends, but
the single malt is bottled at 12 years and has a distinctive full
peaty flavour.

GLENDEVERON

This excellent malt is made in Macduff distillery near the small
town of that name and draws its water from the river Deveron.
Hence the name of the malt.

The distillery, a modern concrete structure, was built by
Brodie Hepburn in 1960 but was sold to Block, Grey & Block,
the whisky exporters, in London. In 1972 it was sold again to
William Lawson of Coatbridge. Lawson was originally a wine
and spirit merchant in Dundee. Glendeveron was off the
market for a short time but is now available as a 12 years old
single malt.

In 1980 William Lawson became part of the General Beverage Corporation, a firm with headquarters in Luxembourg,
which controls the Martini & Rossi organisation.

NORTHERN MALTS

The distilleries producing the Northern malts are situated
along the north-east coast and most of them are north of
Inverness. They will be described rather more briefly than the
Speysides, although some are equally distinguished. It is convenient to travel northwards along the coast, but Glen Mhor
and Tomatin will have to be left to the end for reasons which
will be explained.

DALMORE

This might be described as a good solid dry whisky with slightly peaty flavour, a little reminiscent of Cardhu. The later vintages, however, are less peaty. It is said to mature in the minimum three years, but it is issued from 8 to 20 years old.

Dalmore was founded in 1839 on the site of a famous old meal mill, but was taken over by the Mackenzie family in 1867. They have maintained an active interest in it ever since and, although they merged with Whyte & Mackay in 1967, a descendant of the original family is still on the board.

The distillery has been greatly modernised. The handling of the barley has changed, while the Saladin method of malting and mechanical stoking have been introduced. One of the 1874 stills is in use and with two larger ones the output of the plant has grown enormously.

Dalmore has a wonderful site on the shores of the Cromarty Firth looking across to the Black Isle. At an early date it was fortunate to acquire the sole water rights of the river Alness and can discharge its effluent into the sea.

BALBLAIR

Although Barnard (1887) gives 1790 as the year this distillery was founded, it is claimed that the original distillery at this site was built in 1749, so it is reputed to be one of the oldest in Scotland. It is in the country a few miles west of Glenmorangie with a similar pleasant outlook. In 1840 the distillery was controlled by Andrew Ross & Son but subsequently passed into the hands of the Cumming family, who at one time also had Old Pulteney in Wick. It was bought in 1970 by Hiram Walker.

It was suggested in a previous edition that the taste of the whisky might be 'because the distillery uses a very soft friable peat which may contain a plant responsible for its pleasant unusualness'. However, like most distilleries Balblair no longer does its own malting. The explanation can hardly be correct unless the water picks up this special flavour from the peat through which it flows.

The distillery has a reception centre, but apparently many people go in error to the other Balblair in the Black Isle. Balblair distillery is near Edderton village.

Although the single malt, bottled by Gordon & MacPhail, has been around for some time, A. H. Barclay of Hiram Walker says his firm launched Balblair as a single malt in 1984.

GLENMORANGIE

Glenmorangie is just across the peninsula from Balblair. Distilling began here as a sideline to farming at Morangie, which is about a mile and a half north of Tain. The distillery also has a lovely site looking across the Dornoch Firth to the hills of Sutherland. It was originally a brewery, but was converted in 1842 by William Mathieson and his brother.

The Glenmorangie Distillery Company was formed in 1878 to take over the interests of the Mathieson family. In 1918 the distillery was bought by Macdonald & Muir of Leith, who also own Glen Moray Glenlivet distillery and are blenders.

The water supply is from the Tarlogie springs, which are set in Glenmorangie's own Tarlogie Forest. It is hard and rich in minerals having passed over red sandstone which is unusual since most distilleries favour soft burn water. The spirit stills are also unusual in that they are 16 ft 10¼ in. high, taller than any other in Scotland, which may be a factor in producing the distinctive flavour of the whisky. Charred American oak barrels are used for maturation in order not to mask the flavours too much with wood. All of Glenmorangie's production is retained for bottling as a single malt or for a top dressing to Macdonald & Muir's blended whiskies.

The single malt has become very popular in recent years and is widely available in the UK. Bottled at 10 years and 40% vol, it is light and smooth with a delicate fragrance.

CLYNELISH

The distillery was established in 1819 by the Marquess of Stafford, before he became the Duke of Sutherland, with the idea of using the barley which was grown by his tenant farmers. The family seat, Dunrobin Castle, is on the coast five miles away and is open to the public during the summer.

Clynelish is also near to Brora where coal was mined at one time, but it was of poor quality.

Ainslie & Co, Scotch whisky blenders of Leith, bought the distillery in 1896 and rebuilt it in one year. The Distillers Company eventually became the owners in 1925, and the distillery is now licensed to Ainslie & Heilbron of Glasgow. The subsequent history is somewhat confusing. Clynelish was closed in 1931 in the economic depression and although it restarted again in 1938, work stopped between 1941 and 1945 on account of wartime restrictions on the supply of barley to distillers. A new malt distillery was built on an adjacent site in 1967–8 and this was given the name 'Clynelish'. The old distillery was closed (again) for a time but was reopened as Brora distillery in 1975. Brora was one of the distilleries closed by Distillers in 1983, but whisky at Clynelish is still being produced at the 'new' distillery.

This is good news because the malt has a long-standing reputation. Professor George Saintsbury, the critic and literary historian, wrote about Clynelish in *Notes on a Cellar Book* (1920). He kept his own cask which he regularly topped up from separate jars of his favourite malts: Clyne Lish (*sic*), Smith's Glenlivet, Glen Grant, Talisker, and one of the Islay malts. He added that a friend of his 'held some mixed Clyne Lish and Glenlivet . . . to be the best whisky he had ever drunk'.

Clynelish is certainly the most fully flavoured whisky outside Islay and perhaps the peat mosses from which peat is obtained used to grow seaweed. It is fruity and delicious, and a little like Laphroaig but less peaty. I like it, but it is not to everyone's taste. Bottling is at 12 and 15 years.

OLD PULTENEY

This whisky comes from Wick, the county town of Caithness. It is a whisky of considerable distinction having a succession of flavours and not noticeably peaty. Neil M. Gunn recognised in Old Pulteney when well matured 'some of the strong characteristics of the northern temperament. It has to be come upon as one comes upon a friend and treated with proper respect.' It is a pity that there is not more of it in the south, but it must be remembered that the Scots do not export all their best products.

The distillery, which is the most northerly on the mainland, was opened in 1826 by James Henderson. When Barnard visited it in the 1880s the annual output was about 80,000 gallons, chiefly sold in the provincial towns of England and Scotland. In the hard times after the First World War, the distillery closed in 1926, part of it being used as a meal mill. Sadly it did not reopen until 1951. In 1955 it was sold to Hiram Walker and was completely rebuilt.

The whisky is reputed to be one of the fastest maturing in Scotland and is bottled mainly at 8 years – yet it is still called Old Pulteney. It is also called by some the 'manzanilla of the north'. Excellent though the whisky is, this does stretch the imagination somewhat. It is really necessary to try some and decide for yourself. Some bottlings at 13 years may be found.

GLEN MHOR

From the banks of the Caledonian Canal at Inverness comes Glen Mhor, named after the Great Glen which runs west to Fort William. It is made with water from Loch Ness. Here we have a whisky of real merit made by the Birnie family since 1892. While it cannot be said to have any outstanding flavour it has an honest subtle richness and 'fatness" reminiscent of the patina of old furniture, which it owes to the care with which it is made and the fact that it is so well matured before it is sold. Neil M. Gunn was the resident Excise officer at Glen Mhor from 1923 to 1937 before he resigned to take up full-time writing. He was a great enthusiast for malt whisky and wrote 'until a man has the luck to chance on a perfectly matured malt, he does not really know what whisky is.'

The distillery was one of those closed by the Distillers Company in 1983, so sadly there will be no more Glen Mhor, at least for the time being. It was still listed in 1985 by some of the better outlets, so it may just be worthwhile looking for a bottle left on the shelf somewhere.

TOMATIN

It is a surprise to find a distillery at Tomatin (pronounced like the fruit) 1500 feet high on the northern slopes of the Grampian Mountains about 19 miles south of Inverness. It was based on a fifteenth-century distillery which supplied the needs of men attending the small local market before they and their animals began their long trek south through the hills.

The whisky has an individuality born of local peat and local water which passes through peat over red granite. Unfortunately in a dry year water becomes scarce.

The distillery, which was owned by an independent company, New Tomatin Distillers Co Ltd, was enlarged progressively in the 1950s and 1960s. Twelve new stills were added in 1974 (making 27 in all). The large amount of 'waste' heat was used to warm the water in which eels were reared experimentally for the European market.

Shares of the company were suspended on the London Stock Exchange in 1984 and the company went into voluntary liquidation. It was suggested by *The Times* (22 December 1984) that Tomatin had been hit harder than most distilleries by the fall-off in demand for Scotch. This was because most of its whisky was sold wholesale and the company was therefore severely affected by heavy destocking in the industry in 1983–4. In February 1986 the distillery was bought by two Japanese companies, Tokara Schuzo and Okura, both of which have had trading relationships with Tomatin.

ISLAND MALTS

These malts are not to be confused with the Islay malts which will be described in Chapter 4. The island malts in our present classification are those produced by distilleries which are on islands north of the Highland line. These Highland islands are Orkney on the north and then Skye, Mull, and Jura, on the west coast. Jura, the furthermost south, is in fact very close to Islay.

HIGHLAND PARK

This famous whisky from Kirkwall in the Orkney Islands deserves special mention. When I first tasted it at 40% vol bottled by John Scott, grocer and ironmonger, I was a little disappointed, but later when I obtained the 57% vol I found it entirely different; indeed, it was comparable with the best brandy. Highland Park has always been recognised as one of the best whiskies, no doubt because of the special quality of the Orkney peat.

Kirkwall is the capital of Orkney. It lies on a beautiful land-locked bay. Its narrow streets and picturesque harbour are steeped in the romance of its ancient Viking association, while the town has many ancient buildings, especially the great cathedral of St Magnus, which was built by Durham masons in the twelfth century.

The distillery stands on the hill above the town overlooking Scapa Flow and was established by David Robertson in 1798 on the site of the bothy of the famous smuggler Magnus Eunson. When Robertson died, his brother conveyed the distillery malt barn and other buildings on the site to a Robert Borthwick. After passing through several hands, including those of the Right Reverend Aeneas Chisholm (Roman Catholic Bishop of Aberdeen – acting as a trustee), it became the sole property of James Grant in 1895, under whose name the company continues. His son Walter and his son-in-law Charles Heydon came into the business in 1936. On the death of the latter, Walter Grant became sole proprietor, but one year later he sold the business to Highland Distilleries, though he remained in charge until his death in 1947.

Jim Cryle, marketing manager of Highland Distilleries, stresses that it is the traditional methods of distilling which continue to make Highland Park the distinguished and distinctive whisky it has always been. The distillery does its own malting, but most of the barley comes from other parts of Scotland. The single malt is bottled by the proprietors, James Grant & Co, at 12 years and 40% vol.

SCAPA

Another truly excellent malt is made at Scapa which is two miles north of Kirkwall. A Pictish circle camp over 3000 years old is not far away.

The distillery was built in 1875 by J. T. Townsend, a well-known Speyside distiller. After the First World War the Scapa Distillery Co Ltd was formed, which was bought by the Bloch Brothers. Hiram Walker acquired the distillery in 1954 in the name of their subsidiary Taylor & Ferguson of Glasgow.

Morrice (1983) draws attention to the close historical associations between Scapa and the Royal Navy. During the First World War, naval ratings were billeted there and the distillery was saved from complete destruction by fire as a result of the efforts of the officers and men of the Grand Fleet.

Naval ships are no longer based at Scapa, but the distillery continues to produce its single malt bottled at 8 years.

TALISKER

We now come further south and west, to the romantic Isle of Skye with its single distillery, Talisker. The name comes from Talisker House which was owned by Macleod of Macleod.

The distillery was founded in 1830 by Hugh and Kenneth Macaskill. They had their critics because a former minister of the parish is said to have described 'the erection and establishment of a whisky distillery' at Carbost as 'one of the greatest curses that . . . could befall it or any other place'. In spite of this voice of doom, distilling continued successfully until 1880 when the leaseholder was found guilty on charges of defrauding and went bankrupt. The new owners, Allan & Kemp, were men of substance and the annual output rose to 40,000 gallons. Their partnership was dissolved in 1892 and a company called Dailuaine-Talisker Distilleries Ltd was formed. After further changes the company became a subsidiary of Distillers Company in 1925 and is now licensed to John Walker & Co Ltd.

The distillery is in the charming little village of Carbost on the shores of the beautiful Loch Harport. The village lives for the distillery but most of the men also farm small crofts. A visit to the distillery is worthwhile because it entails a drive across the island with beautiful views of sea lochs and the mountainous Cuillins.

The quality of the whisky was recognised by Robert Louis Stevenson in 1880 when he wrote:

> 'The King o' drinks, as I conceive it,
> Talisker, Islay or Glenlivet'.

Neil Gunn has stated: 'at its best it can be superb but I have known it to adopt the uncertainties of the Skye weather'.

I find Talisker a little less definitive and distinctive than it used to be. Some do not like its light 'oily-like' Irish flavour, or its variety of peatiness, but I do not find it unpleasant. It is bottled at 8 years old and 45% vol. Enthusiasts claim that 'it is a wonderful whisky half-way between an Islay and a Highlander'.

JURA

The Isle of Jura, just north of Islay, is famous for its hills known as the Paps. The first distillery here appears to have been built at the end of the seventeenth century.

In 1810 a new distillery was established and was operated by James Ferguson who owned the machinery, although the buildings were the property of the Campbell family. Photographs and records show that it was a substantial place capable of producing 150,000 gallons, although it is doubtful if it ever did so. There were difficulties with the owners of the site and the distillery closed in 1904.

The present new distillery, which opened in 1963, was designed and built by its first managing director, Delmé Evans, for Scottish & Newcastle Breweries. The distillery is now a subsidiary company of the Waverley Group.

The Isle of Jura single malt at 8 years old was first available in 1974. It is correctly classified as a Highland malt but perhaps has a touch of the Islay flavour.

TOBERMORY

Tobermory is on the Isle of Mull and the first distillery was established in 1823. Barnard (1887) was clearly impressed with the beauty of the site by the sea when he visited it.

The distillery has a chequered history which is too complicated to recount in detail here. Although the Distillers Company took it over in 1916, it closed in 1930. Attempts were made to revive it in 1972. Various business interests were concerned at different times. A very drinkable single malt called Ledaig became available. But after closure between 1976 and 1979 a new company began again and produces a single malt called no longer Ledaig, but Tobermory.

EASTERN MALTS

There are eight distilleries in eastern Scotland, mostly south of Aberdeen, with only two north of that city. North Port was closed in 1983 and in 1985 Glenesk and Glenury Royal were 'mothballed' – this means closed, but with the expectation they could resume production when market conditions improve. So the area has been badly affected by the economic depression and we will only be considering three of the remaining malts.

FETTERCAIRN

This Kincardine distillery is at the eastern end of the Grampians. The original building was established in 1820 by the brothers Guthrie who were born near Brechin. A third brother was the famous divine Dr Thomas Guthrie, a great orator and promoter of temperance and social reforms. He is remembered in Edinburgh by his statue in Princes Street Gardens. In 1824 the distillery was moved to a region nearer Laurencekirk on the picturesque river Esk which supplies its water. The distillery was the first to use oil-heating of the stills.

When the Fettercairn company was first formed in 1887, it had as its chairman Sir John R. Gladstone. He owned the nearby Fasque estates which had been bought in 1829 by John Gladstone, the father of William Ewart Gladstone, the great Liberal Prime Minister, who was responsible for the Spirits Act of 1860. Although this increased duty on spirits, there were some benefits for blenders and subsequently the export of whisky to England was allowed in bottles (rather than casks).

This whisky is, I think, the best of the eastern malts now available, with a full dry flavour. It is bottled under the name Old Fettercairn.

In 1971 the distillery was bought by subsidiaries of Whyte & Mackay Distillers Ltd.

GLEN GARIOCH

The valley of the Garioch has been called the Granary of Aberdeenshire. It begins at Old Meldrum which is the site of the distillery founded, according to Barnard, in 1797. There were various owners over the years. It eventually came under the control of the Distillers Company in 1937. There were, however, a number of difficulties and the distillery was closed in 1968.

Stanley P. Morrison bought it in 1970 and were able by skill and enthusiasm to revive the distillery and produce a 10 years old single malt which has gained a good reputation. Rather a quaint little booklet from the distillery describes the process of whisky making in archaic language. At the conclusion it is stated that 'all efforts to describe the pleasures of GLEN GARIOCH are FUTILE. Be assured, however, that GLEN GARIOCH is SUITED TO ANY MAN'S MOOD and has a TASTE EQUAL TO ANY OCCASION.'

The stills producing this splendid whisky are gas-fired and wasteheat boilers have been installed. Surplus warm water is not wasted, but is used to heat greenhouses in which tomatoes and geraniums are grown.

LOCHNAGAR

This whisky is made at a charming distillery just above Balmoral on Deeside. The name comes from the mountain adjoining the land on which the distillery is built, and the beauty of the scenery was extolled by Lord Byron, who had spent much of his boyhood in the area:

> England: Thy beauties are tame and domestic
> To one who has roved o'er the mountains afar
> Oh for the crags that are wild and majestic
> The steep frowning glories of dark Loch-na-Gar.

The only other distillery on Deeside, called Banks of Dee, was burned down in 1825 by 'those who sympathised with the illicit trade' (Moss & Hume, 1981) following the introduction of the 1823 Excise Act.

The first distillery at Lochnagar was destroyed by fire in 1841, but was rebuilt only to close in 1860. Meanwhile John Begg and his partner built a second distillery nearby which became the new Lochnagar.

A visit by Queen Victoria and Prince Albert, while they were staying at Balmoral, brought the seal of royal approval after they had sampled the product. The accolade given was permission to use the prefix 'Royal'.

The distillery was acquired by John Dewar in 1916 and so became part of DCL in 1925. It is still licensed to John Begg Ltd.

Lochnagar is indeed a wonderful whisky with a subtle flavour of sherry from the cask in which it has been matured – a flavour which cannot be imitated by putting a little sherry in and whisky. It is a privilege to have tasted such a rich whisky. Now much more readily available, it is exported to many important markets of the world. It is reputed to be the second best-selling malt in West Germany.

PERTHSHIRE MALTS

Perthshire has now become part of Tayside Region, but boundary reorganisation – made apparently for convenience of administration – does not seem to be a reason for changing the name of this group of distilleries which are conveniently related geographically.

BLAIR ATHOL

The distillery is not in the village of Blair Athol, but is some 11 miles south on the southern outskirts of Pitlochry which is now well known for its summer festival and its salmon leap.

A Mr Conachar established the distillery in 1826 – he was said to be a descendant of young Conachar who was a companion of the Fair Maid of Perth. Be that as it may, as Barnard writes, the family carried on until the distillery was taken over by Peter MacKenzie & Co in the 1880s. They closed Blair Athol during the slump in the 1920s and this was one of the two distilleries (the other was Dufftown-Glenlivet) acquired by Arthur Bell when he bought the MacKenzie business in 1933. Whisky production did not start again until 1949, by which time Bell's had renewed the buildings in a traditional style.

The distillery is attractively situated on the side of a wooded hill and is beautifully kept. Simon Richmond, Bell's Marketing Service Executive, says modestly there is not a visitors' centre on the scale of some of the Speyside distilleries, but if you turn up at 9.30 a.m. you will be shown round 'informally' (but it is best to check beforehand).

The local Pitlochry water has been considered good enough to dilute the fresh whisky; but in addition there is a much easier supply from the Allt Dour, 'burn of the otter', which passes through the distillery from the lower reaches of Ben Vrackie on its way to the nearby river Tummel.

The single malt, bottled at 8 years, is excellent. It seems at times to have a faint taste of sweetish caramel, but this can hardly be so since all distillers claim that the small amounts of caramel used for colouring can never be tasted. There used to be an old bottling at 80° proof (which would now be 46% vol) which was even better; its fullness and flavour gave it a distinction not commonly found.

TULLIBARDINE

This malt is made near Blackford on the site of an old brewery which is said to have provided ale for the coronation of King James IV at Scone in 1488. The village called Tullibardine is a few miles away north of Gleneagles and Auchterarder.

The present distillery was the work of Delmé Evans and it opened in 1949. After having at least two owners, the distillery became part of Invergordon Distillers Ltd, who also own Deanston, another distillery in Perthshire. The operating company remains the Tullibardine Distillery Co Ltd.

The 10 years old single malt (at 40% vol) has an outstanding almost wine-like flavour. It is no longer available at 46% vol.

GLENTURRET

Like so many Scottish distilleries, Glenturret can claim to be 'one of the oldest' having been founded in 1775. Barnard suggests that smugglers used the site and this often seems to be the case too. The setting in the woods on the west bank of the river Turret, north of Crieff, is certainly beautiful.

In those early years of this century the owners were Mitchell Bros & Co (Belfast) Ltd, but during the depression of the 1920s the distillery closed and the plant and the machinery was removed. A new company was formed in 1957 and a new distillery was built during 1959 and 1960 under the skilful supervision of James Fairlie whose plans were completely successful. The whisky won several competitive awards during the 1970s. In 1981 Glenturret Distillery Ltd became a subsidiary of the French company Cointreau, best known for their liqueurs. It is expected that increased sales in Europe will follow.

The single malt is not yet widely available in England, but it is worth looking for. It is bottled at 8 years, 43% vol.

The distillery has a Heritage Centre which is extremely popular and has large numbers of visitors: it is not very far from Edinburgh and Glasgow.

GLENGOYNE

When Barnard visited this distillery it was called Glenguin and he described it as being 'just below a romantic waterfall 50 feet in height, which supplies all the water used in the works'. For a time the name was changed to Burnfoot and then to Glengoyne which it remains. The distillery can only just be included in this section: it is in Stirlingshire, near Killearn, and although it is just about on the dividing line, it is always classified as a Highland, rather than a Lowland, malt.

The distillery was built in 1833 and was bought by the Lang brothers in 1876. They were wine merchants from the Broomielaw district of Glasgow and had begun blending whisky in the basement of the Argyle Free Church. They eventually took over the whole church and so might be said to have been blending 'the spirit of wine with the spirit divine'.

Glengoyne remained very much a family business until 1965 when the company became part of the Robertson & Baxter group. In the following years modernisation was undertaken, but the distillery remains a showpiece; many of the rooms are tiled and it is all kept beautifully, the character of the buildings being retained.

The 8 years old single malt (40% vol) is readily available and there is also a 15 years old (43% vol) in a special kiln decanter. The whisky is a very pleasant sweetish malt with no outstanding flavour.

4

Islay, Campbeltown and Lowland Malts

There is no particular reason for putting these three types of malts in one group except to balance the rather long chapter on the Highland malts. If the imaginary boundary line were extended westwards into the sea, Islay would lie to the north of it, but its malts are so distinct that they must be considered separately. Campbeltown and the Lowland malts belong south of the line.

ISLAY

This beautiful, remote island is in the Atlantic to the west of the Mull of Kintyre and up until recently had eight active distilleries – but two have closed in recent years.

The Islay malts have all got something special about them and they may be described as powerful, but no longer is it permissible in this day and age to say that they are whiskies exclusively for men. They do have an aggressive, peaty flavour. Many people say they taste 'medicinal', especially Laphroaig; so much so that some find them pungent and unpleasant. Nonetheless they do have devoted followers amongst serious whisky drinkers. Maybe the taste can be acquired with practice, so those who are put off by their first sip should persevere. Whether or not you like them, it is undoubtedly true that these malts add flavour to many popular blends.

The contribution of the island to whisky is unique and its history gives some insight into this phenomenon. Daniel Campbell became Laird of Islay early in the eighteenth century. He was Member of Parliament for Glasgow Burghs and in 1727 he voted for the extension of the malt tax to Scotland. This was so unpopular that an angry mob in Glasgow ransacked his town house. He was awarded £9000 in compensation (a lot of money in those days), and with this he was able to complete the purchase of Islay. He set about transforming the unproductive heath of the island into fertile arable land and in 1767 his family planned the new town of Bowmore. A curious fact emerges which perhaps explains why whisky making was profitable in the island. For some strange reason, Islay (and nowhere else) was exempt from the activities of the Scottish Board of Excise which had been set up in 1707. The duties of Excise were handed over to the Laird, which provided a powerful incentive to the Campbells to encourage distilling. He had to pay only a small sum to the government for this 'peculiar privilege' and the unusual concession was not withdrawn until 1797. The full version of this story has been recorded in a booklet published by Bowmore Distillery.

LAPHROAIG

This is the outstanding whisky of Islay and, although it may not be liked by everyone, there are some who will drink none other. Its 'iodine-like' taste may have been an advantage in the 1920s when there was an American market for medicinal whisky during Prohibition (Moss & Hume, 1981).

The distillery (pronounced 'Lafroyg'), which is white-washed, stands on the seashore in a small bay protected by rocky islands. The original buildings were associated with a farm and were put up by the Johnston family in 1815. An incident in the early days suggests it really is possible to have too much of a good thing, because one of the managers died after falling into his burnt ale vat. The family ran the distillery for many years, but in 1962 Seager Evans bought a 25 per cent stake and completed the purchase by 1972 when the name Seager Evans had changed to Long John International. One point deserves special mention: the distillery was managed by a woman which is unusual in Scotland, especially for a distillery which has been said to produce a 'man's whisky'. Miss Bessie Williamson (later Mrs Campbell) became Secretary and Director of the company in 1950. She subsequently became Managing Director in 1954.

The single malt is available bottled at 10 years and 43% vol and also at 15 years, 40% vol. The strong flavour is not from the barley as most of this comes from the mainland. The island has an abundance of rain and acres and acres of peat. It is the peat which is probably responsible for the characteristic, and instantly recognisable, taste.

LAGAVULIN

There has always been rivalry and dispute between Lagavulin and nearby Laphroaig which even reached the point of litigation in the distant past.

Lagavulin means Mill in the Valley and the distillery is 3 miles east on the road leaving Port Ellen, passing Laphroaig on the way. The ruins of Dun-naomhaig Castle, stronghold of the Lords of the Isles in the twelfth century, stands prominently on a neighbouring peninsula.

The first mention of the distillery is in the local records of 1742 when it was nothing more than a series of bothies owned by the Johnston family who were engaged in smuggling whisky to the mainland. They were succeeded by the Grahams who entered into partnership with J. L. Mackie & Co, who were the proprietors when Barnard visited the distillery. Mackie became White Horse Distillers who are now a subsidiary of the Distillers Company.

The single malt, 12 years old and 43% vol, is certainly less 'strong' than Laphroaig, and perhaps for this reason is rather more popular.

ARDBEG

Ardbeg is the fourth distillery on the south-east coast of Islay and is only a short distance east from Lagavulin. It was established in 1815 by the MacDougall family and as with so many other places the site was originally used by smugglers. After a number of changes in ownership, Hiram Walker acquired the entire shareholding in 1979.

Although the single malt is on both Milroy's and Gordon & MacPhail's lists, the distillery was closed in 1981 and there is no indication when it will reopen.

BRUICHLADDICH

It is hard to imagine a distillery on a better site than Bruichladdich, which lies on the east coast of the great bay called Loch Indaal, and is opposite Bowmore.

The small distillery was built in 1881, but went through some bad times before being bought by A. B. Grant, a blender and exporter, of Glasgow. He completely modernised it and output was increased.

The single malt is a typical Islay whisky, rich and pleasant, without the 'medicinal' quality of Laphroaig. It is bottled now at 10 years old, 43% vol, and there is a 15 years old available in a special decanter.

BOWMORE

The distillery is in the chief town of the island, and stands on a shelf overlooking Loch Indaal. It was built in 1779 by Hector Simson and looks almost like a fortress, with an imposing gateway. The next owners, from 1837, were William & James Mutter; James must have been a remarkable character, because not only did he expand the distillery and manage three farms in Islay, but was also 'Ottoman, Portuguese and Brazilian Vice-Consul' in Glasgow. J. B. Sherriff bought the distillery for £20,000 in 1925, but he chose a bad time and Bowmore was closed down. During the Second World War, the distillery became a base for Coastal Command Sunderland and Catalina flying boat squadrons. William Grigor & Son Ltd of Inverness took over in 1950 and began to restore the distillery. Things began to move more rapidly after Stanley P. Morrison Ltd bought Bowmore in 1963. Production was expanded and the bicentenary was celebrated in 1979 with a special malt bottled in an elegant flask. The distillery held a competition in 1981 for the best design for an ideal malt whisky glass. The winner was Rosa Branson and her glass is based on the thistle pattern, but the shape is quite distinctive and good to look at and drink from.

The standard 12 years old 40% vol Bowmore has a powerful yet delicious, fruity flavour and is less peaty than other Islay malts. It certainly is one of my favourites.

CAOL ILA

The remaining two distilleries on Islay are on the east coast facing Jura across the Sound of Islay, which stretch of water is called Caol Ila in Gaelic.

This distillery was noted only briefly in the third edition but was described as a 'gem'. Founded in 1846, it was acquired by Bulloch Lade & Co in 1863 and subsequently became a subsidiary of the Distillers Company.

The single malt really is a collector's item, but it is bottled by Gordon & MacPhail at 18 years and has all the good qualities of Islay whisky.

BUNNAHABHAIN

The distillery was built in 1881 and owned by the Islay Distillery Company. When this company combined with Glenrothes in 1887 the Highland Distilleries Company was formed.

Like Caol Ila the malt is not easy to come by, but Gordon & MacPhail have a 1965 bottling. A special decanter was produced in 1981 to celebrate the centenary of the distillery.

CAMPBELTOWN MALTS

The story of the disappearance of thirty-two distilleries in Campbeltown is not only sad, but may even be a warning for the present. At the beginning of the century the little Royal Burgh at the south end of the Kintyre Peninsula was the whisky capital of Scotland. From the point of view of whisky making Campbeltown was ideal. It had good supplies of water, coal and peat and in the early days much of its barley was grown locally. It is a surprise to see so much arable land so far west, but no doubt the Gulf Stream makes it warmer than it otherwise would be. 'Success, however, contains the seeds of destruction', for some distilleries began to put poor spirit into poor casks to satisfy the rapidly growing population of Glasgow and its whisky speculators.

There was a time when the Campbeltown malts were known as the Hector of the West, the deepest voice of the choir – a compliment indeed. When the financial slump came in the late 1920s the public and the blenders became more choosy and turned up their noses at the Campbeltown 'stinking fish', especially when plenty of good whisky from the Highlands was available. We must only hope that the tragic story of Campbeltown does not repeat itself elsewhere. Thirty years ago twelve distilleries remained but today there is only one working distillery: Springbank.

Campbeltown looks a long way away on the map but the journey there by car from Tarbert at the top of Loch Fyne is well worthwhile. The town itself is of historic interest. It is said that, in the region of Parliament Square, Fergus, the first King of Scotland, built his Parliament House in 503. Tradition has it that the Stone of Destiny, on which the Kings of Scotland were crowned, came from here. It was subsequently removed from Scone to Westminster Abbey by Edward I of England.

SPRINGBANK

The distillery was built in 1823 in Campbeltown and was later acquired by the Mitchell family whose descendants still own the business. In spite of extensive modernisation, the traditional method of floor malting is still used. There are two spirit stills, one of which is used for redistillation of foreshots and feints. Another unusual feature is that this distillery is the only one of two, the other being Glenfiddich, to bottle their own malts.

Springbank is a very pleasant full-flavoured whisky which is available at various ages and strengths (from 8 to 19 years and 46% vol to 57% vol).

GLEN SCOTIA

This whisky is very different from Springbank, being heavier, strongly flavoured and somewhat reminiscent of an 'oily' Irish whiskey. The same peat is used in both distilleries, and the water for both comes from Crosshill Loch, and so the difference which might account for the different taste is likely to be the separate distillation of foreshots at Springbank.

The distillery was built in 1832 in the town centre and has changed hands many times. Morrice (1983) recounts that one of the earliest owners, 'a certain McCullum, drowned himself in a nearby loch on realising that he had been done out of a large sum of money by swindlers whom he met on a sea cruise'. His ghost is said still to haunt the distillery.

The present managers are Gillies & Co of Glasgow, who became a subsidiary of Amalgamated Distilled Products in 1970. Much of the whisky goes for blending but the single malt is bottled at 5 and 8 years at 40% vol. Work was stopped in 1984 (see ADP in Chapter 11).

LOWLAND MALTS

The Lowland malts were the first whiskies to be drunk in quantity in England. They are more gentle than the Highland malts and are said to mature more quickly. Around 1850 most larger towns in the south of Scotland had a distillery. Yet today there is not even one in Dumfries where Robert Burns was an Exciseman and wrote many of his poems. In 1906 there were two distilleries in Langholm, one in Annan and seven in Lanarkshire. All have disappeared.

More single Lowland malts are available than there used to be, but much of the whisky, particularly from the distilleries near Edinburgh and Glasgow, goes for blending.

BLADNOCH

Bladnoch distillery has a pleasant site on a bank of the Bladnoch river from whence it draws its water. It is about one mile south of Wigtown, the county town of one of the least spoiled districts in Britain. The distillery was opened by the McClelland family in 1818 and for many years it flourished, but like so many small distilleries it fell on evil days in the 1930s and closed down. In 1956 the somewhat derelict premises were revived by the Bladnoch Distillery Company. It was sold again in 1964 to McGowan & Cameron, blenders and wholesalers of Glasgow. They had difficulties and in 1973 Inver House Distillers Ltd (a subsidiary of Publicker Industries USA) became the owners. The distillery closed again in 1980, but was bought by Bell's in 1983 and production was started after complete renovation of the plant.

In its heyday this was a particularly good whisky and I had some which was 30 years old and which had a wonderful bouquet. The present 8 years bottling has been disappointing and it remains to be seen whether Bell's can work any magic with it.

LADYBURN

William Grant & Sons Ltd built a new grain distillery at Girvan in the early 1960s and subsequently added the Lady-burn Malt Distillery. The site is spectacular and looks across the sea to Ailsa Craig with the Isle of Arran in the background.

Most of the whisky goes for blending, but as with Glenkin-chie, Wm. Cadenhead bottle a single malt, 14 years old and 45% vol, thought to be rather disappointing by some experts.

If we cross the Clyde between Glasgow and Greenock we reach the beautiful county of Dumbarton, which lies between Loch Long and Loch Lomond. The southernmost peaks of the Grampians can be seen from the Kirkpatrick hills which are between Glasgow and Dumbarton. The county is partly Lowland and partly Highland; indeed, it is on the imaginary Highland Line which runs from Dundee to Greenock dividing the Highlands from the Lowlands.

The whiskies are quite different from the Highland malts, yet not quite Lowland malts. Whisky has been made in this area from the earliest days, but many distilleries have disappeared. Most goes for blending and three single malts are available on the retail market: Auchentoshan, Littlemill and Rosebank.

AUCHENTOSHAN

The glen in which Auchentoshan distillery is situated overlooks the river Clyde near the Erskine Bridge. It was founded about 1800 and was owned by the MacLachlans for the first sixty years of this century. During the Second World War it was the only distillery to be bombed and the stream is said to have run with blazing whisky. After being part of the Bass Charrington group, it was bought by Eadie Cairns in 1974 and they sold out to Stanley P. Morrison in July 1984.

The single malt is triple distilled and has a delightful and rather unusual flavour. Its quality has been recognised by a Gold Award from the Club Oenologique. It is on the market from 5 to 8 years old, 40% vol. The older whisky, from 12 years onwards, is in a rectangular bottle.

LITTLEMILL

Littlemill is at Bowling near the town of Dumbarton in a most delightful situation. At one time, it is said, beer was made here for the monks of Paisley Abbey 'across the water'.

The distillery was built in about 1750 by George Buchanan, a maltster from Glasgow, and was greatly enlarged by a Mr Hay in 1875. There were then a number of owners, but the distillery was closed during the depression of 1929 to be reopened in 1931 by Cecil Fausett and Duncan G. Thomas, who was an American of 'Scottish origin. The distillery was bought by Barton Brands of Chicago and Kentucky, and now Barton Distilling (Scotland) Ltd is a subsidiary of the large Amalgamated Distilled Products Ltd.

The old bottlings of the single malt have the lovely brandy flavour of a Lowland malt. It has been on the market as young as 5 years when it is rather disappointing, but it is now also available at 8 years and is more mellow at this age. The best old whiskies may be taken up rapidly by blenders and if this is so it is a pity, because the reputation of any distillery depends on having available fully matured samples of its products.

The distillery is now (1985) closed, at least temporarily.

Finally, there are two other Lowland malts which merit description. The first is made at Rosebank distillery, about 20 miles due west of Edinburgh, and the second at Glenkinchie, which is a slightly shorter distance to the south-east.

ROSEBANK

This is an excellent light-flavoured whisky, somewhat reminiscent of Glenmorangie. It used to be described as a 'silent malt'. It is easy to understand why such a light whisky was preferred in England to the old and sterner Highland malts before modern blends became available; although modern Highland malts, when matured, are very different from their predecessors.

Rosebank is on the banks of the old Forth and Clyde canal, about one mile north of Falkirk. As early as 1798 distilling was carried out in this area by the Stark Brothers, but in 1840 the distillery became the property of the Rankine family, who reconditioned it in 1864. This has again been done by the Distillers Company.

A visit to Rosebank makes an interesting trip, especially if we cross from the south by the Forth Bridge, and recross the river 15 miles further up by the Kincardine Bridge, visiting on the way the historic village of Culross, beautifully restored by the National Trust for Scotland.

GLENKINCHIE

The distillery is one of the showpieces of the Distillers Company and now houses a Museum of Malt Whisky Production – it is important to check the opening times as it was closed during July and August (1985).

Glenkinchie is near Pentcaitland in East Lothian and is easily reached from Edinburgh, but signposting is poor and the distillery is quite difficult to find. It is in a glen and the Lammermuir Hills are immediately to the south. The distillery has its own attractive garden and it is unusual in that it still has a farm attached to it.

Distilling began in 1837 and has continued, with breaks only for war, ever since. John Haig Ltd now hold the licence. Most of the whisky goes for blending but a single malt is on the market, although not easy to obtain – it can be bought at Milroy's, but not Harrods or Fortnum & Mason. It is bottled at 13 years old, 45% vol, by William Cadenhead of Aberdeen.

5

The Vatted Malts

A description of vatted malts may hardly seem to warrant a chapter to itself, but this particular kind of whisky does lie between the single malts and the blends, which use grain whisky and which we will be coming to in the next chapter.

The history of blending really goes back to vatting which has been done for many years. Vatting consists of mixing together single malts of different ages made at different times of the year. This definition, which comes from Sir Robert Bruce Lockhart's book on Scotch, is a little more informative than the strict Oxford English Dictionary which describes 'vatted' merely as 'placed or stored in a vat; said esp. of wine'. Vatting was carried out in some pot-still (malt) distilleries and indeed we have seen how Glenfiddich add some 12 years old malt to their standard 8 years old single malt.

Whisky drinkers have often experimented themselves by mixing different malts together, and Professor Saintsbury's practice of topping up the cask which he kept in his cellar with different malts has already been mentioned (p.48).

Ushers of Edinburgh are credited with being the first to produce a vatted malt, which they did in 1853 when they produced Old Vatted Glenlivet, and others followed their lead. It is, for example, known that Walkers sold Cardhu Vatted Malt in the 1890s.

Bottled vatted malts are now produced on quite a large scale and perhaps a somewhat extended definition is needed. At present a vatted malt, as it is bought, consists of a mixture of single malts probably from different distilleries. The precise recipes are the secret of the 'vatters' and it is impossible (with few exceptions) to find out exactly what the constituents of any individual vatted malt are.

Why then should this be done? It might possibly be a matter of cost. The cheapest whisky is grain whisky, which is rarely drunk on its own. The most expensive is a well-matured single malt. A blend uses a variable amount of grain whisky mixed with a variable number of malts: it is relatively inexpensive. A vatted malt is likely to cost as much as an 8 or 10 years old single malt: but less than a 12 or 15 years old, and probably less than a de luxe blend. The argument almost becomes circular but merchants have felt the market need for vatted malts. Those of the best quality may give the age of the malts used, but this is not always the case.

One could not say that since young malts are cheaper (by virtue of less time spent in store) they may be included in some vatted malts. Who knows? – except those who do the vatting and the pricing. It is true, though, that a vatted malt labelled 8 years will contain no single malts of a lesser age.

One of the better vatted malts is undoubtedly Strathconon produced by Buchanan and consisting of four 12 year old malts. But Gordon & MacPhail have also bottled some very special vatted malts: 25 year old malts to celebrate the Queen's Silver Jubilee and vatting of Glenburgie, Glen Grant and Strathisla 'distilled in 1948 and 1961' to celebrate the marriage of the Prince of Wales to Lady Diana Spencer. They also have other high class vatted malts such as Pride of Strathspey 25 years old, Pride of Orkney 12 years old and so on. There is no doubt these are the genuine article, much sought after, and not easy to obtain out of Scotland: although Milroy's has Pride of the Lowlands (also 12 years old). Other superior vatted malts are Glenforres (12 years old – William Whiteley) and Glenleven (12 years old – John Haig). Rather younger at 8 years are Mar Lodge (Findlaters), Glen Drummond (Saccone & Speed) and Glencoe (R. N. MacDonald) – the latter at 51% vol. These are not cheap whiskies and they are worth drinking.

Just as some mass retail shops (like Spar and Tesco) have

their own ordinary blends, Harrods has its Pure Malt blend and the Army and Navy Stores have their 7 year old Fine Old Vatted Malt.

There are, however, some slightly curious specimens. Sheep Dip marketed by M. J. Dowdeswell & Co Ltd of Oldbury-on-Severn, Bristol, is described on the label as an 8 years old malt, but it is in fact vatted and bottled by George Morton of Montrose. It is possible to imagine reasons why a farmer might find it convenient to order a case of sheep dip: it might even pass, to some jokers, as a tax-deductable expense.

Another odd vatted malt is Duart Castle marketed by Whigham's of Ayr and mostly exported. It is named after Lord Maclean's home on Mull with his permission. Tobermory is the only distillery on Mull, but as Morrice (1983) points out, there is no obvious connection between it and Duart Castle which is certainly not a distillery. Cooper (1983) draws attention to the only vatted malt from the Outer Isles – 5 years old Poitdubh which is intended as a 'good everyday malt for the local community'.

It is as well to look at vatted malts with some circumspection. What, for example, is one to expect from Peter J. Russell's Seven Stills 5 years old 100%? The reputation of the bottler and the price are the only guide for the tiro, otherwise you must try and see if you like it. If the word single is not on the label of the malt you buy, then remember the whisky may be vatted.

Commercial vatted malts are now here to stay and there seems little doubt they satisfy a need as there is a demand for them. Many will, however, prefer to stay with what they know best – their favourite single malts.

6

Visiting Distilleries

Certainly it does not seem to be necessary
for any distiller, Highland or Lowland,
to cloud his activities in mystery.
JAMES ROSS, *Whisky*, 1970

It is hoped that readers of this book will become sufficiently
interested in whisky to wish to visit one or two distilleries. This
could certainly provide an excuse to see some of the most
beautiful parts of Scotland. For the enthusiastic tiro the Whisky
Trail on Speyside provides an easy introduction. A pamphlet
produced by the North East of Scotland Coordinating Committee for Tourism and the Scottish Tourist Board gives all
the information about opening times and so on. The route,
about 70 miles long, is clearly signposted with an attractive
logo. The use of the word 'trail' has to be forgiven since it is
difficult to find a descriptive substitute. The distilleries on the
trail are best approached from the south by way of Aviemore
and Grantown-on-Spey. Incidentally, the Whisky Centre and
Museum at Inverdruie, Aviemore, is worth a brief stop. The
premises are in rather an unprepossessing hut, but there is a
good selection of whiskies and books on the subject. There is a
small museum, an audiovisual show and a tasting room.
　　The distilleries on the trail are:

> Tamdhu
> Glen Grant
> Strathisla
> Glenfiddich

The Glenlivet
Glenfarclas

These are all well worth visiting, but it is probably best to limit yourself to two or three a day. If you want to attempt the whole trail it may be best to find a hotel in Grantown, which is 12 miles south, or in one of the towns on the trail itself, such as Craigellachie, Rothes, Dufftown or Tomintoul. These are all small Highland towns or villages which have their own attractions – wide streets with solid granite houses and magnificent scenery.

Tamnavulin is on the road in the southern part of the circuit and has recently opened a reception centre. Cardhu, which is near Tamdhu, hopes to have a centre open by 1986.

The distilleries themselves have usually retained their attractive pagoda roofs although these are largely decoration, because the malting kilns are rarely used nowadays. The appearance of the buildings varies, some being pleasant to look at (Strathisla, for example), but rows of large warehouses make others look rather like factories displaced into the countryside. As you drive around you will see many distilleries – there are, for example, 11 on the 37 miles of road between Grantown and Elgin. Architecturally, two buildings in the district are interesting to look at. Tormore, built in 1958–9, is a curious mixture of postwar modernism and the local vernacular. On the other hand, Allt à Bhainne, five miles south of Dufftown, is quite uncompromising in its starkness, but sits remarkably well in the rugged landscape. The Braes of Glenlivet in the same area was also built by Seagram in a similar style. Unfortunately, neither distillery is open to the public.

Most distilleries, including those on the trail, are open between Easter and the beginning of the autumn. Skiers in the Cairngorms, if frustrated by the weather, may like to know that Glenfiddich and Glenfarclas are open in the winter.

The pattern of each visit is much the same and could prove exhausting for the faint-hearted. After a welcome you are usually invited to see a video or a slide-tape presentation. These are all of high quality: Glenfiddich uses three projectors with a fourth on a side-wall with spectacular effect. Then follows a tour of the distillery itself, usually in groups of 10 people, with a guide who may be a student. Although the basic ingredients are the same – mash house, washbacks and stills – there are many interesting variations. Nearly always special provision for visitors has been made with wide access, so it is rarely necessary to clamber up and down narrow steps. Finally a free dram is often given in the reception centre. A strategically placed shop provides whisky and souvenirs of various kinds. A word about miniatures may be relevant here. Any serious whisky drinker would think of buying only a full bottle of anything, but if you do this all round the trail it will cost about £100. Although you will have tasted the whisky in each distillery, these small bottles do provide a convenient and economical way of finding out what you like without paying £12 or so for a bottle which you may not want to finish (although this seems an unlikely possibility).

The Whisky Castle at Tomintoul, which is on the trail road, and the Whisky Centre at Aviemore, have large selections (as does Gordon & MacPhail in Elgin).

Other distilleries on Speyside or thereabouts with reception centres are Glenburgie, Glendronach and Miltonduff.

If all this seems too much, and it will be for some people, and if you happen to be in Edinburgh or Glasgow for some other purpose, then you should consider a visit to Glenturret. This is just to the north-east of Crieff and between 50 and 60 miles from each of the major cities. The distillery is small and has made a great effort to cater for visitors. The audiovisual show comes after the tour and the attached museum is excellent – a small charge is made for these 'extras'.

Islay is a splendid place for a holiday, and of the distilleries there, Bowmore has a reception centre, but Bruichladdich, Bunnahabhain, Laphroaig and Lagavulin will receive visitors by appointment. The same applies to Highland Park and Scapa in Orkney.

In the Aberdeen area, Glen Garioch has a reception centre; so do Blair Athol, near Pitlochry, and Glengoyne in Stirlingshire;

in the Lowlands there are Auchentoshan, north-west of Glasgow, and Glenkinchie, east of Edinburgh.

Many distilleries are 'silent' in July and sometimes August. This period of closure is traditional and in the early days when distilling was very much connected with farming, the distilleries shut so that the workers could help with the harvest. Even at this time, when maintenance work is carried out, a visit is well worth while. It is interesting to be able to peer into the mash tuns and the stills, although you do miss the excitement of seeing the fast flow of what is to become whisky through the spirit safe. Opening times vary so it is important to check before visiting, but the question is how to find the telephone numbers if you are not in the district. It is well worth buying *Scotland's Distilleries: a visitor's guide*. This does not appear to have a named author, but is published and printed in Scotland by Famedram Ltd of Gartochan, Alexandria, Dumbartonshire. Brief details are given of 108 malt distilleries. The cost is modest and it is hoped that it will be brought up to date regularly.

We should be grateful to those distilleries where visitors are cheerfully welcomed and where, presumably, the management believes that it is a valuable public relations exercise. Two of those on the trail on Speyside have remained in the hands of the original owners (Glenfarclas and Glenfiddich), while three others are owned by Seagram (The Glenlivet, Strathisla and Glen Grant), and the remaining one, Tamdhu, belongs to Highland Distilleries.

The Distillers Company is making a reception centre at Cardhu which may join the trail. The company also has a museum at Glenkinchie, but this is closed in July and August, which shows little regard for the tourist trade. Bell's, who have a centre at Blair Athol, appear to concentrate their efforts on the trade rather than the consumer.

Visitors should not become too much of a nuisance and perhaps an optimum number of reception centres has now been reached. Nonetheless, anyone with a special interest can be sure of a warm welcome and a fascinating opportunity of discussing with an expert the finer points of whisky making.

7

Grain Whisky

Grain whisky is lighter in weight and less distinctive in taste than malt whisky . . . but it is wrong to describe it as a neutral spirit.

ROBERT BRUCE LOCKHART, *Scotch*, 1967

Grain whisky, as we have seen, is made from maize and – by law – from malted barley in a patent-still. It does not have the full flavour of malt whisky, it takes less time to mature and is much cheaper to make. The reasons for this will become clear when the methods of making malt whisky in a pot-still and grain whisky in a patent-still are described in Chapter 8.

Unlike malt distilling, grain distilling is of relatively recent origin and a convenient date to remember is 1826. This was when Robert Stein, who had a distillery at Kilbagie between Clackmannan and Kincardine, took out a patent for a still which he had devised to produce alcohol in a single operation as opposed to the two distillations used in a pot-still. Stein's still was known as a patent-still, but it was superseded by an improved design produced by Aeneas Coffey in Dublin in 1830.

This did not mean that the Stein family had failed in any way as distillers. Rather the opposite; and we need to look farther back, and forward, to see why. An important factor was their connection with the Haig family, one of whose forebears had been a farmer and, like so many farmers, had carried out some distilling in the seventeenth century. In 1751 Margaret Stein married John Haig and two of the pioneering families in Lowland distilling were thus united. John Haig died of a sudden heart attack when he was only 53 – leaving five sons to be educated. They were sent to their uncle Robert Stein at Kilbagie to learn distilling. Four of the boys ran distilleries of their own and at one time all the surviving Lowland distilleries belonged to the Stein and the Haig families. The ramifications of the two families and the distilleries they owned are complicated, but the relevant connection with the making of grain whisky can be summarised. James, who was John Haig's eldest son, began distilling at Canonmills in 1782. This was taken over by the Steins, but the Haigs built new distilleries at Lochrin and Sunbury, near Edinburgh. It was John Haig, son of William and grandson of the John who married Margaret Stein, who started the Cameronbridge distillery in 1824. Shortly afterwards he installed a new patent-still which was, as we have seen, invented by his cousin Robert Stein. Although malt spirit had originally been produced at Cameronbridge more and more of the cheaper grain spirit was made.

The Steins were the first regular exporters of whisky to London and much of their spirit was converted into gin and other forms of alcohol. However, grain whisky began to be drunk by itself in England and demand increased dramatically, particularly when grain was mixed with malt to make a blend. Many grain distilleries were established in Scotland after 1860 and posed a threat to the many, much smaller, Highland distillers. At the same time the Lowland distillers felt threatened particularly because they were restricted to use grain, whereas their counterparts in England were allowed other raw materials to make their spirit. In 1856 the six leading Lowland firms entered into an agreement to share their trade amongst themselves in fixed proportions. This was the group which became the Distillers Company, which will be described in Chapter 11.

WHAT IS WHISKY?

The manufacture of whisky from corn (then, of course, in the pot-still) had been prohibited in 1796 and it was subsequently claimed that the term 'Scotch whisky' should be confined to that made from malted barley. After the invention of the patent-still and the growth of grain distilleries, large quantities of grain whisky were being sold in London as Scotch whisky. The duty was negligible, and it was anyway much cheaper than malt whisky. This disturbed the Highland malt distillers who failed in their attempts to get Parliament to ban what they regarded as 'trash'.

The matter was brought to a head in a curious way and it does not seem quite clear why the London Borough of Islington (as opposed to any other authority) should have chosen, in 1905, to prosecute publicans for selling as whisky 'articles not of the nature, substance and quality demanded'. It is true that the previous year they had been successful in prosecuting producers of 'fraudulent' brandy, but they had much more difficulty with their 'What is Whisky?' case. Vested interests were involved in what really turned out to be a malt versus grain contest. At this time the Distillers Company had been formed and they were able to use all their power to support the case for grain whisky.

The first hearing was at the North London Police Court when Mr Davidge, a local publican, was charged with having sold 'to the prejudice of the purchaser, who demanded Scotch whiskey, something which was not of the nature, substance and quality of Scotch whiskey'. (Notice at that time whisky was spelt with an 'e'). The magistrate came to the conclusions which favoured the malt distillers since he said that 'patent still spirit alone is not whiskey'. His decision seems to have been based on evidence from the Public Analyst of Islington, Dr Teed, who had said that 'whiskey should consist of spirit distilled in a pot-still derived from malted barley . . .'. The convicted publican appealed, but after seven hearings the quarter sessions at Clerkenwell were unable to reach agreement.

The controversy continued and after a good deal of delay, with pressure from both the Islington Borough Council and the Distillers Company, the President of the Board of Trade agreed to the appointment of a Royal Commission in 1907. The whole affair was brought to a head when the Distillers Company put an advertisement in the *Daily Mail* for pure bottled grain whisky from their Cambus distillery. The Royal Commission was under the chairmanship of Lord James of Hereford, and there were six scientific and medical experts. Their terms of reference were essentially to consider whether restrictions should be placed on 'the materials and processes' used in making whisky and whether there should be a 'minimum period during which any such spirit should be matured in bond'.

The committee heard evidence during 1908 and 1909 from many witnesses. This time Dr Teed did not carry so much weight, particularly as he seemed to rely on Robert Burns for evidence, but it is a relief to find that Dr Schidrowitz could not arrive at a chemical definition of whisky and believed that it was not possible to be sure of the effects of certain constituents, although measurable, on flavour.

The conclusions of the Commission were reported in 1909 and can be summarised as follows:

(a) That the name 'whiskey' should *not* be restricted to the product of the pot-still.

(b) That whiskey was a spirit obtained from a mash of cereal grains saccharified by the diastase of malt.

(c) That since the trade in whiskey seemed to be honestly and fairly conducted, there was no need for any special legislation.

Furthermore, no minimum period was laid down for bonding.

The most important outcome was a legal definition of Scotch Whisky, to the great benefit of the producer and the consumer. It subsequently became possible to make and distribute blended whisky on a larger scale at cheaper cost to meet increasing demand. This was greatly to the advantage of the development of the industry as a whole.

SUBSEQUENT LEGISLATION

It was not until 1915 when the Immature Spirits Act became

law that whisky had to be kept in bond, i.e. matured, for at least two years. Curiously enough this was introduced by Lloyd George who allowed himself to be convinced that cheap 'new' whisky was responsible for the drunkenness which he wished to control. A year later the period was increased from two to three years. This created a shortage of supply and a steep rise in the cost of the whisky.

This may be the point to move right up to date and to give the current definition of whisky. It clearly is important to get this right, especially in relation to which spirits (exported or made abroad) can be called whisky. The following paragraphs are quoted from a booklet issued by the Scotch Whisky Association. By their very nature, they do not make for easy reading but they are legally precise and correct:

Scotch Whisky has been defined in law since 1909. The definition is to be found in the Finance Act 1969, Schedule 7, paragraph 1. This was amended in 1979 and 1980 to take account of the introduction of the system of alcoholic strength measurement recommended by the International Organisation of Legal Metrology and the requirement that maturation must take place in Scotland. Current British legislation states that:

(a) the expression 'whisky' or 'whiskey' shall mean spirits which have been distilled from a mash of cereals which have been –

   (i)   saccharified by the diastase of malt contained therein with or without other natural diastases approved for the purpose by the Commissioners; and

  (ii) fermented by action of yeast; and

 (iii) distilled at an alcoholic strength (computed in accordance with section 2 of the Alcoholic Liquor Duties Act 1979) less than 94.8 per cent in such a way that the distillate has an aroma and flavour derived from the materials used, and which have been matured in wooden casks in warehouse for a period of at least three years.

(b) the expression 'Scotch Whisky' shall mean whisky which has been distilled and matured in Scotland and the expression 'Irish Whiskey' shall mean whiskey which has been distilled and matured in the Republic of Ireland or in Northern Ireland or partly in one and partly in the other;

(c) the expression 'blended whisky', 'blended whiskey', 'blended Scotch whisky' or 'blended Irish Whiskey' shall mean a blend of a number of distillates each of which separately is entitled to the description whisky, whiskey, Scotch Whisky or Irish Whiskey as the case may be.

(d) the period for which any blended whisky, blended whiskey, blended Scotch Whisky or blended Irish Whiskey shall be treated as having been matured shall be taken to be that applicable in the case of the most recently distilled of the spirits contained in the blend.

With these definitions out of the way we can return to grain whisky before going on to the art and business of blending.

IS GRAIN WHISKY DRINKABLE?

Neil Gunn's opinion in his classic *Whisky and Scotland* (1935) that 'the product of the patent still is almost pure alcohol, flavourless and mainly used for industrial purposes' is a little harsh, but contains more than a grain of truth. He was probably not correct in his assertion that grain whisky was used for industrial purposes. Industrial alcohol was originally made (in separate distilleries) from surplus whisky. By the 1930s it was being made from molasses and today from petrol. It also seems unlikely that grain whisky, or gin spirit, would be pure enough to use for 'scientific purposes'. Gunn was a single malt enthusiast and so might be held to be prejudiced on this issue, but the fact is that single grain whisky is not a widely marketed drink. There is only one variety available, Choice Old Cameron Brig, still made at John Haig's original distillery at Cameronbridge in Fife. It is 40% vol and costs the same as an average blend. I had rather expected that it would be harsh and tasteless, but I find it a reasonable drink especially when well matured. I have also been given a sample of grain whisky made at Invergordon which was quite pleasant to drink.

Grain whisky is not 'silent', as has often been suggested, and it 'assures a liveliness and freshness that would otherwise be missing' in a blended whisky, according to George Shortreed, who was the Master Blender at Justerini & Brooks. So let us accept that, although a good malt is the heart of a good blend, the grain provides the body: it certainly does so quantitively as we shall see.

PRODUCTION OF GRAIN WHISKY

The method of making grain whisky will be discussed in Chapter 8, but it is now relevant to give some indication of the amount of grain whisky which is produced to fulfil the need for blended whisky.

There are probably about 100 working malt whisky distilleries, and much of what they make goes for blending, yet there are only 10 grain distilleries. The Distillers Company have, as we have seen, closed or 'moth-balled' quite a number of malt distilleries, and they have closed one grain distillery (Carsebridge). A list of working grain distilleries would include:

Cameronbridge	
Caledonian	
Cambus	Distillers Company
Port Dundas	
North British	North British Distillery Co
Dumbarton	Hiram Walker International
Strathclyde	Long John International
Invergordon	Invergordon Distillers
Girvan	William Grant & Sons

These distilleries make far more grain whisky than the malt distilleries make malt whisky which is a reflection on the ease of production. The figures fluctuate from year to year, particularly in times of depression, but a comparison made at random of two years, 1978 (high production) and 1985 (low production), gives some idea of relative output:

	MALT	GRAIN	TOTAL
1978	209	250	459
1985	105	155	260

The figures are given in approximate *millions* of litres of pure alcohol.

In spite of its widespread manufacture grain whisky, as such, is exported in only relatively small quantities.

8

The Making of Whisky

*Distilling is the art of separating, or
drawing off, the spirituous, aqueous
and oleaginous parts of a mixed body
from the grosser, and more terrestrial
parts by means of fire, and condensing
them again by cold.*

A. COOPER,
The Complete Distiller, 1803

The qualities of grain and various malt whiskies have now
been discussed and it is time to see how they are made. The
account will not be technical in any way, but it is worthwhile
trying to grasp the essentials of the various processes which are
used. Certainly this chapter should be read carefully before
visiting a distillery, and indeed again afterwards since it is often
easier to appreciate the description of a place or a process after
one has actually seen it. Diligent travellers will read their
guide-book before their journey, but will enjoy it more and
understand it better after they get home.

Although the last chapter was concerned with grain whisky it
seems more logical to consider malt whisky first since histor-
ically it was made before grain. Furthermore the process is
more interesting and subtle.

MALT WHISKY

The basic steps in making malt whisky are: first, malting the barley; second, fermenting an extract of the malt with yeast; third, driving off the flavoured alcohol by heat. The process is illustrated by the diagram on p.88 which should be looked at while reading the text.

Malting (diagram A) is the process by which the barley seeds are made to germinate by moistening them and then keeping them at an appropriate temperature (about 16°C). The first step is to *steep* the barley in water for two or three days. Next comes the controlled drying. The traditional method was to spread the 'steeps' on the concrete floor of the malting house, which is a large dimly lit building with a low ceiling. The process of germination is encouraged by turning the barley at regular intervals. Men using large wooden shovels used to do this and progress slowly from one end of the room to the other. *Floor malting* is hard work and needs a good deal of space, so it is rarely used nowadays, though it can be seen at Balvenie. The process can take 8–14 days.

Alternative methods of malting have consequently been devised. *Saladin boxes* were introduced into many distilleries in the 1950s. These had been invented by a Frenchman of that name, and consist of long narrow concrete or metal containers in which the steeped barley is spread. It is then aerated by a series of large metal screws arranged transversely, which travel slowly up and down the length of the box (although the word box is used it is perhaps not a good choice since the top is open). The atmosphere in the building is warm and damp to encourage germination. The time taken is about seven days and so it is quicker than floor malting. Many companies now use large malting *drums* which revolve slowly, and air is blown through them to control the temperature. Other more sophisticated techniques have been introduced in recent years.

Whatever method is used, germination is stopped when rootlets have developed. If it were allowed to proceed further, the seed would use up its supply of maltose: this happens normally in the soil before the root and leaves have begun to take up nutrient. At the end of malting, the barley has produced

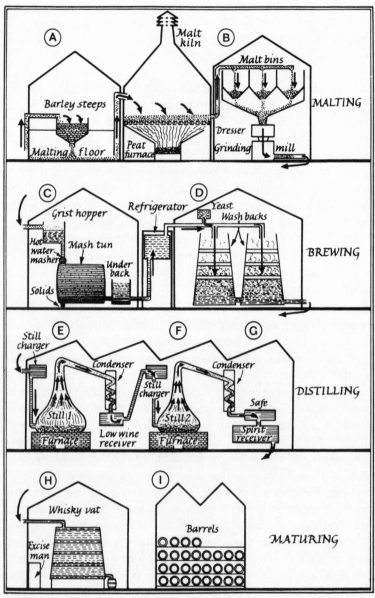

Diagram of a distillery: in many distilleries malt is purchased from maltsters

the maximum amount of the enzyme diastase, which makes the starch soluble, so the grains become soft. A small amount of maltose (a sugar) is also produced.

Drying and peating (diagram B). The kiln, with a pagoda-like ventilator at its top, was the characteristic building of all old distilleries and was where the germinated barley was dried. The barley, now called *green malt*, is spread over the perforated floor of the kiln. The furnace below used always to be stoked with peat alone, but now more often coke is used and some peat is added to it. The smoke percolates through the drying green malt and this imparts a flavour to it which may be apparent in the whisky when it is finally made. Drying takes about two days. The green malt becomes crisp and friable and is pleasant to taste.

Mashing and brewing (diagram C). When the prepared malt is needed it is first passed through a dresser to remove the dead rootlets and any foreign material, such as stones or nails. If anything metal were included, it might produce sparks with a risk of fire at the next stage. This is when the malt is coarsely ground in a mill, and is converted into *grist*. The grist is mixed with water, from the distillery's own supply, in a large round metal vat call the *mash tun*, whose capacity may be from about 9000 to 36,000 litres (2000-8000 gallons). Mashing takes about eight hours and the malting action of the diastase begins again, converting the remaining starch to maltose and other fermentable sugars. When the water has dissolved most of the maltose from the barley grist, the fluid (called *wort*) is drained off through the perforated bottom of the mash tun to a *worts receiver* or *underback* is carried out and repeated washings ensure that no maltose is wasted. The solid residue remaining, known as *draff* or *grains*, is removed, processed elsewhere and sold to farmers for cattle food.

Fermentation (diagram D). The wort is cooled and pumped into *washbacks*. These are tall covered vats which usually stand on the floor of the room below the working floor. The capacity varies from 5000 to 50,000 litres. Washbacks used to be made of wood: Oregon pine, Douglas fir or larch were common. It is conceivable that this might contribute something to the taste of the whisky, but maintenance is a problem and nowadays stainless steel is usually preferred, although many wooden ones are still in use. Yeast is added and fermentation begins: the enzymes converting the maltose to alcohol and carbon dioxide. The process is vigorous and the froth is removed from the top of the fluid by mechanically operated paddles. So far the process is very like brewing beer, indeed the man in charge is known as the brewer. After about forty hours or so, the end product is a clear liquid known as *wash* and consists of water, yeast and about 7% alcohol per volume. The next stage is to separate the alcohol from the wash by distillation.

Distillation (diagram E, F, G). When the wash is heated, the alcohol, being more volatile than steam, is driven off first and is collected by condensation. This seems simple enough, and in whisky-making the procedure is carried out in a *pot-still* which is a large onion-shaped vessel (see opposite page) made of copper, and with a long narrow neck leading to a condensing coil or *worm*.

Heat is applied in a variety of ways, either externally or internally, the method differing from one distillery to another. Originally a peat fire was used, but then a coal or coak furnace, often mechanically stoked, became the commonest method. This applied heat directly to the outside of the base of the still. Steam provided by central oil, gas or coal-fired boilers is also used to heat coils or 'kettles' in the still. Some stills have insulating jackets over their lower half to conserve heat. There are two separate stages, each of which has its own still:

The interior of a modern distillery showing the wash and low wines stills. Commonly the condensers are on the outside of the building. (Drawn from a photograph of Glenglassaugh Distillery by kind permission of Highland Distilleries Ltd)

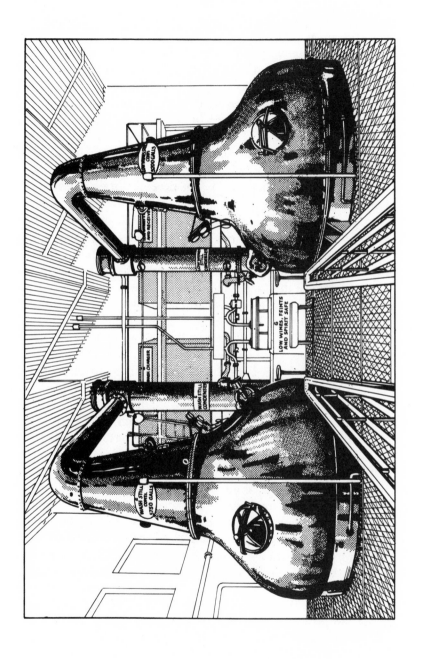

(a) *The wash run* (diagram E). The wash is heated slowly in the still until it vaporises. The alcohol is driven off and condenses in the worm which is surrounded by cold water in the worm tub. The fluid recovered is known as *low wines* and has an alcohol content of about 25%. The bottom of a coal-fired still is scraped by a copper chain with rotating arms called a *rummager*. About 11,000 litres of wash produce about 2500 litres of low wines which is stored in the low wines receiver before the next stage. The wash run takes about six hours and the temperature is carefully controlled.

(b) *The spirit run* (diagram F). The process is then repeated in a similar, but often slightly smaller, still. This run may last from four to six hours and it is only the middle of the flow, the *heart of the run* or the *middle cut*, which has the required strength and quality for malt whisky: it will have an alcoholic content of about 70%. The first part of the run produces the *fore-shots* and the last part are the *feints* which contain the heavier elements, such as fusel oil. The fore-shots and feints are fed back into the wash still for redistillation in the next batch. No alcohol is wasted. Whatever is finally left in the low wines still, the *spent lees*, is little more than water and passes to a treatment plant before being discharged as effluent, usually into a neighbouring river. Any residue in the spirit vat, called *pot ale* or *burnt ale* is removed and used for cattle food or fertiliser.

The spirit safe (diagram G) through which all liquid from both stills passes is a key part of the operation. It is essentially a glass box, usually set in brass, or in stainless steel in modern distilleries. The old-fashioned brass type is a splendid-looking piece of equipment and is an easily recognisable part of the still house. It is secured by Customs & Excise locks and the stillman has to work without being able to touch his product, let alone taste it. By turning the appropriate taps the flow of the distillate can be bypassed into a cylindrical vessel inside the safe. Its temperature and specific gravity can then be measured. Water can be dripped into it to see whether or not cloudiness develops. The wash run goes through quickly, but the choice of the 'heart of the run' from the spirit still is absolutely critical and it is in making this discrimination that the stillman uses his skill. Too much of the fore-shots or the feints might spoil that particular batch of whisky, which would then have to go for redistillation. Remember that he makes his decision using a no-touch technique and it is a responsible job demanding loving care with an element of ingrained intuition. Although automation can certainly simplify the procedures, it is unlikely that electronic wizardry will ever be able to define the heart of the run as effectively as the stillman, and the spirit safe is still present in modern distilleries.

The spirit has a strength of about 75% alcohol and is quite clear when it leaves the spirit still. It is reduced in concentration by 10-15 per cent by the addition of process water and is stored in a vat (diagram H) before being put into casks.

Maturation (diagram I). The freshly made spirit is undrinkable and by law has to mature for at least three years before it can legally be called whisky. It is therefore poured into oak casks and allowed to lie in a bonded warehouse. The most commonly used cask is a hogshead (250 litres), but there is also a barrel (180 litres) or a butt (500 litres).

During the process of maturation, the whisky loses a small amount of alcohol and water by evaporation each year. This is known light-heartedly as the *angel's share*. The climate of the warehouse is important and in a wet season the whisky loses strength, whereas in a dry season it loses bulk. The Excise allow a loss of 3 per cent a year. As time passes the whisky becomes smoother and less toxic. It is not known exactly what happens chemically, but these beneficial changes cannot be hurried.

The stages in whisky-making, which have been described, can be summarised as follows:

(a)	Malting	Steeps	3 days
		Maltings	10 days
		Kiln	2 days
		Mill	2 hours
(b)	Mashing	Mash Tun	8 hours
(c)	Fermentation	Wash Back	2 days

(d) Distillation   Wash Still   6 hours
                     Spirit Still   6 hours
(e) Maturation   Wooden Casks   5–15 years

The times given are only approximate and will vary in each distillery, and there are gaps at times between the various stages. It is probably true to say that from the time mashing starts, the whisky is made in about 5 days and maturation takes 5–15 years.

Labour. Working under the supervision of a manager, the brewer and the stillman are the two most important people in the distillery. Remarkably little labour is needed and quite a large distillery may employ only 20 or 30 people, but since many are situated in remote areas this is a sizeable proportion of local village life. Consequently the many closures in recent years have been disruptive to local society. More modern automated distilleries will need even fewer men.

Excise. Although the Exciseman cannot play a constructive part, his presence in the distillery affects the process of whisky making and ensures that everything is meticulously checked. The numerous pipes in the working areas are painted different colours to make his job easier: red is for wash, blue for low wines and black for the clear spirit. In the past, every distillery had its own resident Exciseman but since the Rayner recommendations were accepted in 1982, conditions have been relaxed somewhat. There is now a revenue assistant, colloquially known as the *watcher*, in each establishment, and a senior Excise officer will cover several distilleries.

VARIATIONS IN MALT WHISKIES

The characteristics, especially the flavour, of individual malt whiskies can be related only to the ingredients and the method of making. Certainly Scotch whisky is not what it used to be since many of the impurities which gave it 'fire', and gave rise to hangovers, have been removed. It is now no longer necessary to add honey, heather tips or gorse flavourings to improve the taste.

There remains a good deal of doubt about the significance of a number of variables which may be relevant. The following paragraphs will discuss some possibilities, but they will raise more questions than they will answer.

Water. Most malt whisky is made in the Highlands of Scotland where the beautiful scenery is often obscured by rain. There is certainly plenty of water about and many consider that this is responsible for the quality of the whisky. The water is good to drink by itself and its softness makes it also good to wash in. Water *running off granite and through peat* is said to be the best for making whisky. But granite is an insoluble substance and probably cannot contribute much as the water does not stay on it for very long. One excellent and popular malt whisky prides itself on using hard water which runs over red sandstone. Soft water is undoubtedly a better solvent than hard and so it could more easily dissolve substances other than maltose from the malt mash. It might well be that these substances are responsible for some of the characteristic taste of malt whisky. There is something rather mysterious about it all and perhaps it is best not to ask if acid rain is affecting the situation today.

Barley. The prime ingredient must be important, but perhaps less so than was formerly supposed. In the early days distillers used the barley grown in their neighbourhood and it was bought in quite small quantities. Highland barley contains more fat and protein which contributes to its fruitiness, but at the same time makes a heavier whisky which takes longer to mature. On the other hand, barley from Lothian and England is rich in starch which produces a high yield of alcohol and a lighter whisky which matures more quickly. Therefore the modern practice of using such barley produces a whisky which is more acceptable to modern taste.

Nowadays most distilleries buy in barley which has already

been malted elsewhere. Precise specifications are laid down, but it seems likely that some of the individual characteristics introduced into the whisky at this stage may be lost.

Peat. This material, now well known to gardeners in England, has for many years been used for domestic fuel in parts of Scotland and Ireland. It is decayed vegetation which usually comes from marshy land and is made of various mosses and marsh, heath and moorland plants. Quality varies depending on the different types of vegetation and its depth. It may be in layers 3-5 feet deep and it used commonly to be cut by hand. At its best it is hard and dark when dried, but it may be soft and friable.

Since the best water for making whisky runs through peat, it is possible that peat might contribute something to the taste of whisky at this stage.

Of more importance might be the effect of the peat used in the kilns. The smoke has a characteristic aroma which transmits a flavour to the drying barley and so through to the whisky. This may be less prominent when malted barley is produced in bulk by specialist maltsters and bought in by the distillery. The Islay distilleries all use the double peating method in their malt kilns which produces a malt with an enhanced 'peat-reek'. This could account for the recognisable similarity of their flavour. Perhaps seaweed is incorporated in the peat, producing the 'medicinal' taste.

The stills. We now come to an interesting, but somewhat speculative, discussion on the way the process of distillation may be affected by the stills themselves.

First, there is their size and shape. It is claimed that small or large stills each will produce spirit of differing tastes. Although the shape has been described as 'onion-like', some have straighter sides and wider necks. The column may be taller or shorter, more or less tapering, or have a bulge (boil-pot) near its base. Many distillers are convinced that the physical attributes of their stills do impart character, but it is not clear how this is so.

Second, the way the stills are fired is likely to also have some influence. Some distillers believe that direct firing of the still improves the flavour of the whisky because of the extra 'cooking' at the bottom of the still. In any case, the still is heated slowly so that in a sense the wash is 'stewed' before the alcohol and water vapour come off. The nature of the fuel used is only likely to be important in so far as it influences the rate and duration of the process. Heating by internal steam coils is said to alter the character of the whisky. But again the evidence is largely empirical.

Heart of the run. The way this is chosen is critical. The heavier elements in the low wines are largely discarded, but some need to be retained as these provide a depth of taste which is not present in the pure spirit. Since this is done by human hand there will be variations which could account for variations in taste which can be found in different bottles of the same malt. This can occur, but every care is taken to ensure that it does not happen. Obviously the vatting of a number of casks will mask a bad 'run', if there ever is one, and vatting the same malt at different ages will also eliminate the risk. Certainly the blender would find life very difficult if there was much variation in the product of individual distilleries.

Maturation. There are three important aspects in the process of maturation which affect the final product.

First, the *cask*. Sherry casks were always used in the past. They were readily available since they had been used to import sherry to England and they were the cheapest the Scots could buy. Now they are scarce, but some distilleries use them exclusively. They contribute a sweetness which helps to develop a well-rounded blend and also make the whisky become darker over the years. Oak Bourbon casks are sometimes used. One distiller believes that the bourbon, and charring, leaches the wood flavours from the oak and prefers to avoid whatever it is that sherry casks put into the whisky. This is quite contrary to the distiller who swears by oloroso sherry casks. Others will vat together whisky of the same year of distillation, some of which has been matured in sherry and some of which matured in plain oak casks. In general, American oak appears to be thought the best wood. If old sherry casks are wanted, but cannot be obtained, then oak casks can be treated with sherry which is allowed to stain the wood before filling with whisky. Nowadays, a cheaper substitute called 'pajarete' can be used for this purpose.

The casks are valuable and, if well cared for, may last even a hundred years. Most distilleries employ their own cooper who looks after the casks, repairing and remaking them when necessary.

Second, the *environment* in which the casks are stored influences the effects of maturation. The cool damp climate in the Highlands seems ideal and presumably this is why distillers prefer to keep their whisky in their own warehouses even though it may have already been sold.

Third, the period of '*sleep*' – the time spent in the cask – is important. Whisky improves as it ages and it becomes darker with time as it takes more colour from the wood. A young malt of, say, 5 years of age will be paler and more fiery than a 15 year old. The colour can be changed by a tasteless additive, but the smoothness and other subtle qualities can be acquired only by waiting. Colour in itself does not relate to the taste or strength. Fashion may dictate the need for lighter whiskies, in colour and in body, and these will need less time for maturation.

Maturation takes place more quickly in smaller casks and this has to be balanced against storage costs.

All whiskies are not at their best at the same age, so samples are nosed or even tasted during maturation. Some malts are drinkable at 8 years, but at present 12 years is regarded as the optimum. Others will continue to improve up to 25 years which inevitably makes them more expensive. Probably little is ever gained beyond 25 years and indeed whisky is thought to lose some of its quality after this time.

Bottling. Whisky is chill-filtered before bottling with the object of removing any slight cloudiness which is present or may occur when water is added: this the consumer would not like. Some experts, including the founders of the Scotch Malt Whisky Society, believe that this process removes 'something' and that the taste of a single malt is better if it is not carried out. The other thing that happens at this stage is that water is added to bring the strength of the whisky in the bottle to the required level, usually 40% vol. Since whisky is not bottled at distilleries, except for Glenfiddich and Springbank, the water added presumably comes out of the local tap. Excellent though this may be, it is different from the water with which the whisky was made. Relatively little is used and it seems unlikely that this could make any substantial difference to the taste. Nevertheless, this was one of the reasons put forward by Highland Distilleries when they obtained an injunction in 1983 to prevent Gordon & MacPhail from bottling Bunnahabhain without their authorisation. There are other elements in this legal action, because 'authorised' bottlers in, say, Glasgow presumably use their own water. The Gordon & MacPhail case will be mentioned later: but at present judgement is pending. Perhaps it is worth noting that the Scotch Malt Whisky Society do not dilute the whisky they bottle which is issued at various strengths from 56% vol to 64% vol.

It is said that whisky does not 'change' once it is bottled, although it is said to 'brandify'. This word is not in the *Shorter Oxford English Dictionary*, but presumably means 'becomes like brandy'. This may explain why three standard malts which I have had in the bottle for 35 years tasted better than new examples of the same brand. What is certain is that if dregs (say, one-quarter of the contents) are left in a bottle for more than a year or two, it will go cloudy and lose its taste. So if you open a bottle, it should be finished within a reasonable time. I would not wish to experiment to try to find out how much can be left for how long. If you want to collect malt whiskies it is better to keep the labels rather than keeping almost-empty bottles.

THE MYSTIQUE OF WHISKY MAKING

When all the possible causes for the variations in flavour of different malt whiskies have been considered, there remains a subtle mysterious 'something' which cannot be described even by the makers. Their methods have developed over many years and must be the result of empiricism. Although malt whisky from an individual distillery may vary a little from time to time, this is hardly surprising since the makers may not taste their product in its final form for 15 to 20 years. The stillman's experience does seem to be critical, but presumably even this step might be controlled by a correctly programmed computer. But whilst maturation is necessary, all the good whisky may have been drunk before the new product arrives.

Scientists have analysed the process, so there is some understanding of its nature. But most agree that whisky making is an art (or should it be a craft?) since purely scientific methods have not been successful and nobody has been able to make anything equal to Scotch whisky outside Scotland. There are many imponderables, but most of us are quite happy to accept that there is an element of mystique, which seems preferable to knowing that our favourite drink could be made by chemists in a laboratory. Walter Bagehot, the Victorian political writer, advised 'Do not let in daylight upon magic'. He was referring to the monarchy: perhaps this applies to malt whisky as well.

GRAIN WHISKY

Less need be said about the making of grain whisky: the process is quicker, cheaper and not so interesting as the pot still. It is carried out on a much larger scale in a smaller number of distilleries situated around Edinburgh and Glasgow. The exception is at Invergordon which was built to provide employment in northernmost Scotland.

A brief account of the development of the *patent still* first by

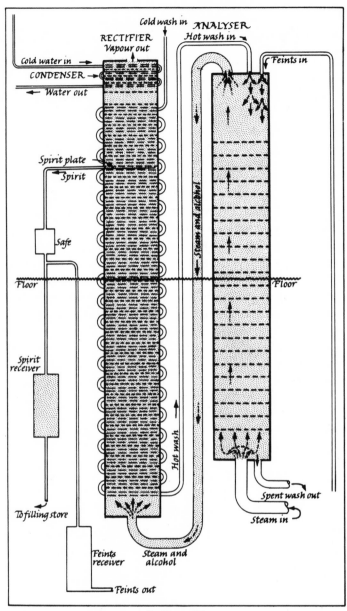

Coffey still

Robert Stein and then by Aeneas Coffey has been given in Chapter 7.

A mixture of maize and barley is used. The maize is finely ground and the starch gelatinised by steam. About 15 per cent of malted barley is added to the mash tun to provide the diastase which converts the starch to maltose. The wort is cooled and then pumped into large wash-backs which may hold as much as 180,000 litres. Yeast is added and fermentation begins. So far the principles of the process are similar, except in scale and in the use of maize, to that in the malt distillery. The next step is different as the distillation is carried out in the *Coffey still*. These are two huge columns, each 40 feet tall. The first is the *rectifier* and the second the *analyser*. The original stills were made of wood, but now metal is always used. The diagram (p.101) shows the arrangement reading, as it were, from left to right. The wash goes in at one end and trickles over a series of perforated trays, through which steam is driven from below. The steam drives off the alcohol, while the cold wash as it enters cools the alcohol which is then condensed by a cold water coil at the top of the rectifying column. There is an ingenious arrangement by which the first and last parts of the distillate are redistilled.

The great advantage of the Coffey still is that it can work continuously so long as wort and steam are available, and it requires much less labour than the traditional pot still. This way of making alcohol is a chemical industrial process involving considerable accuracy. The product is remarkably pure as the wash is not stewed as in pot distilling. It is controlled by the Excise by way of a spirit safe.

Grain whisky has to be kept for at least three years, and because it reaches a peak of maturity earlier than malts, it is commonly used within a year or two of that time.

9

The Business of Blending

*'They gave evidence that there was
increased demand for a whisky of a milder
kind and the blends of pot still and
patent still whisky were in large
demand by the consumer . . .'*
Select Committee of the
House of Commons, 1891

What is now called 'blending' began with the 'vatting' of
different malts as described in Chapter 5. This started in about
1853 when Usher's of Edinburgh, who were agents for Smith's
Glenlivet whiskies, mixed several malts together, some no
doubt better than others, to make Usher's Old Vatted Glenlivet Whisky. The idea may have come from France where the
shortage of brandy after the phylloxera epidemic led to what
might be regarded as the eking out of supplies by mixing old
and new together. The situation was quite different in Scotland, but Usher's no doubt added considerably to the amount
of Glenlivet whiskies available and they achieved a more
consistent product.

RISE OF BLENDED WHISKY

Derek Cooper (1983) suggests that it was commercial ex-
pediency which led Scotch whisky merchants to realise that
'there would be a substantial economic advantage in mixing
grain whisky with the more expensive and mercurial products

of the pot still'. This somewhat cynical view may be basically true and certainly blending was initially intended to reduce the cost of a well-flavoured whisky. But the energetic Scotsmen who introduced their whisky into England were able to do so because they had a product of consistent quality. Consumers wanted whisky (perhaps to replace their brandy and soda) and they knew what they would get if they ordered a reputable brand. Good-quality blended whisky certainly came increasingly in demand during the latter half of the nineteenth century, first in the UK and then throughout the world. This was the basis for Scotland's greatest export industry and was a real success story (Chapter 10).

WHAT IS IN A BLEND?

The immediate answer is that nobody but the blender knows which whiskies go into blends, and in what proportions. These are closely guarded trade secrets, although it is possible to make some assumptions. It is on the whole likely that a blending company which also owns distilleries will use their own malts in their blends. Bell's blends could be presumed to contain at least some malts from Blair Athol, Dufftown-Glenlivet, Pittyvaich, Inchgower and Bladnoch. Other similar examples could be given and when we discuss individual blending companies in a later chapter, the distilleries they own will be listed. These subtleties will not be of great interest to the ordinary drinker but he may like to wonder whether he can recognise, for example, the distinctive taste of Lagavulin in White Horse whisky. Many different malts are made which are used only for blending and are never seen as bottled single malts, such as Glen Spey, Glentauchers, Loch Lomond, Pittyvaich, to name a few.

A standard blend may contain as many as 30 or 40 different malts and perhaps six or seven different grain whiskies: the differences will be of both kind and age. The complexity of the mixture seems quite remarkable. Blenders who own distilleries will exchange their whiskies for others from other distilleries and money may not change hands. Nevertheless, the bringing together of so many whiskies in one place would seem to be an expensive business and one may well wonder why it is done. The basic reason seems to be the need to achieve a uniform product which can be maintained indefinitely. There may be an element of basic statistics here: the larger the number of items the more likely is the outcome of the analysis to be significant. This cannot seriously be applied to the problem in hand, but some say that the large numbers are a safeguard for the blender. If any malt disappears from the market, temporarily or even permanently (and this is quite likely in these days when distilleries do close), then the blend can be balanced again with less difficulty than if only three or four varieties were involved. It seems certain that when blending started there were fewer constituents, but the large numbers seem here to stay.

It may, however, be important to know the proportion between malt and grain whisky in any given blend. We have seen that grain is not entirely silent and that it is relatively cheap. In the early days the proportion was probably about half-and-half, but David Daiches (1980) suggests that in the so-called standard blend there is probably 60 per cent grain to 40 per cent malt. Wallace Milroy puts the proportion slightly higher: two-thirds grain to one-third malt. But the cheaper the whisky the more grain spirit it will contain. It is possible that some brands may contain as much as 80 per cent grain and so can be said only to be flavoured with malt. It would be very sad if the reputation of whisky were to suffer in the drive to reduce its price. But basically you pay for what you get.

THE BLENDER'S NOSE

Blending is an art which depends on a sense of smell rather than taste. Samples of different whiskies are 'nosed', usually in a glass somewhat like a sherry copita, by the blender. Tasting, followed by spitting out, is rarely necessary.

Jim Milne, who is now Justerini & Brooks' Master Blender, gave us a brief demonstration at their Blythswood plant near Glasgow. There was an obvious difference between the smell of a 1 year old and a 5 years old grain whisky. Similarly a 5 years old Speyside malt could clearly be distinguished from a 10 years old sample from the same distillery. An Islay malt was easy to identify. The difficulty is to recognise the different aromas, let alone the taste, within a blend. What needs years of experience is to nose a whisky in the process of blending and to recognise what is missing, and harder still to know exactly what to add to put it right. Samples have to be taken on different occasions to be sure that the correct result will be obtained.

The physical process of blending is in itself quite straightforward. The different whiskies, which have been maturing for a number of years, are assembled according to the magic formula of the particular blend. Each is opened and nosed. If it meets the requirements it is closed and the same process is carried out for the other constituents. The blending itself takes place by rolling each cask over a long trough and opening it so that its contents flow into a large vat. The whiskies are mixed by currents of air flowing through them. Some blenders mix the malts first and subsequently add the grain. When all is done, the whiskies are usually 'married' in oak casks for at least a year so that they can mature further and interact with each other.

CONSUMER'S CHOICE

The consumer is bewildered by the choice available, and while it is reasonable to experiment, it may be best to stick to the brands you know. The most popular at home are Bell's, Teacher's, Haig and Famous Grouse, but abroad Johnnie Walker Red Label, J & B Rare and Dewar's are in the lead.

The large number of brands seem more likely to reflect the effort by companies in advertising in different countries, rather than the consumer's taste. We shall discuss whisky tasting later, but at this point it is relevant to report a test carried out by *Which?* magazine in 1979. Ninety Scottish men and women who were all regular whisky drinkers made up the panel. The whiskies were either a leading brand (Bell's, Haig or Teacher's) or a cheap brand (Augustus Barnett's Special Scotch, Claymore, Glenside–Peter Dominic, Robertson's Yellow Label, Sainsbury's). Each member of the panel was given four different whiskies to taste and they were not able to tell whether they were drinking a well-known or a cheap brand. There was no evidence to suggest that the cheaper brands were less liked than the well-known brands. This is surprising because I have from time to time tried drinking cheaper whisky, even with soda, and have always been disappointed and not thought the economy worth while (and having no vested interest this was disappointing too). The precise details of the *Which?* tests were not published in the magazine and it would be helpful to have the opinion of an expert who is used to setting up trials of this type for assessing drug treatment. It would also be necessary to have a statistical analysis to show the true significance of the results. But perhaps this is taking it all too seriously. My own preference, which is subjective and varies from time to time, is: Haig, White Horse, Famous Grouse, J & B Rare.

Many 'de luxe' whiskies are on the market and are distinguished from the cheaper standard blends by the amount of malt whisky used, together with the age and quality of the individual malts. Age in fact is often given on the label and if, say, 12 years is stated this means that no whisky in the blend will be younger than this. It is true that words like 'choice', 'very old', 'liqueur' (nowadays usually avoided), and 'rare' appear to be used somewhat indiscriminately and the adjective may seem to apply to the label and a fancy bottle rather than the contents. Nonetheless, many of these whiskies really are excellent and worth the extra money which they cost. It is invidious to select examples, but well-established 12 years old superior blends are Antiquary, Chivas Regal, Dimple Haig, and Johnnie Walker Black Label. Once again this type of whisky has failed to pass the *Which?* test. As far back as 1970, the Consumers' Association reported that their panel, who sampled well-known standard blends and 'de luxe' whiskies, did not find one preferable to the other. Once more it is a matter of trying for yourself: drink what you like best and what you can reasonably afford, but I would prefer to be given, say, a bottle of Chivas Regal than a bottle of Johnnie Walker Red Label.

To conclude this brief review of blended whiskies a quotation from David Daiches (1980) is appropriate: 'The reputable blended Scotch whiskies are sound and pleasant drinks, if not as interesting, as individual or as flavoursome as a pure malt whisky.'

10

The Creation of a Wider Market

*The vast whisky fortunes were to be
made, not by the original Highland
distillers, but by the traders and blenders.*
ROBERT BRUCE LOCKHART, *Scotch*, 1967

The demand for blended whisky began during the last years of
Queen Victoria's reign. But it took a small group of enterprising Scotsmen to seize the opportunity open to them to market
whisky on a large scale in the United Kingdom and throughout
the world. They were the people who were responsible for
satisfying the demand and they were able to create business
empires whose names became household words. Their companies exist today, although in the 1920s and 1930s they
became subsidiaries of the great Distillers Company.

The men were fascinating characters and their names are:

John Haig of Cameronbridge
John Dewar and his sons: Sir John (Lord Forteviot)
 and Sir Thomas (Lord Dewar)
Alexander Walker and his sons: George and
 Sir Alexander
James Buchanan (Lord Woolavington)
William Sanderson
Sir Peter Mackie

The Distillers Company Ltd was generally referred to as
'DCL' until it re-registered its name as 'The Distillers Company PLC' to comply with the Companies Act, 1980. The use of

the abbreviation in connection with the Company's subsequent history may not be strictly correct, but it is so familiar that it is retained here for convenience.

JOHN HAIG

The Haig family played a great part in the early days of the patent still and the introduction of grain whisky (p.78) when they were closely associated with the family of Stein. The Haigs were originally border farmers, the first of whom there is any record being Petrus del Hage, whose name appears in a charter between 1162 and 1166. He was descended from a Norman knight who came over here with the Conqueror in 1066, and was eventually given the lands of Bemersyde which have been in the family ever since.

The branch which began distilling were farmers in Stirlingshire and, as was the custom, produced whisky for their family and friends as a sideline. In 1655 Robert Haig got into trouble with the local kirk for working his still on a Sunday.

John Haig had married Margaret Stein in 1751 and they had five sons, all of whom were involved in whisky making. The youngest, William, had two sons, John and Robert. It was this John Haig who built a distillery at Cameronbridge in 1824. The family firm was founded with its headquarters at Markinch. There were various amalgamations, but the company was finally acquired by DCL in 1919.

The Haigs had even managed to establish a connection with Irish whiskey because the first John's eldest daughter married John Jameson who founded the famous firm of John Jameson & Son at Bow Street Distillery, Dublin, in 1780. Another member of the family had established in Glasgow an export business of Haig & Haig which sold, especially in America, under the brand names of 'Haig & Haig' and 'Pinch'. This firm was badly hit by Prohibition in the United States (1919–33), and joined the Distillers Company in 1923, before becoming a wholly owned subsidiary of John Haig & Co Ltd in 1925. It no longer exists as a separate entity.

John Haig of Cameronbridge was one of the original direc-
tors of DCL at its foundation. One of his sons was its first
Company Secretary and another was the originator of 'DCL
Yeast'. The youngest became a Field Marshal. This was
Douglas Haig, born in 1861, who served in Sudan, South Africa
and India and finally became Commander-in-Chief of the
British Army in France during the First World War. He was
created Earl Haig of Bemersyde for his services. He had little
time to devote to the family's business affairs, but he was
Chairman of the company and a Director of the Distillers
Company for some years before his death in 1928.

Blending and bottling of Haig stopped at Markinch in 1983
when work was transferred to a more modern plant at nearby
Leven.

John Haig whisky has a delicious after-flavour which lingers
on the palate and makes it my favourite blend. The de luxe
'Dimple' in its characteristic bottle stands out amongst whiskies. The company also markets a vatted malt, Glenleven.
Bottlings from their malt distilleries at Glenkinchie and Glen-
lossie have been made by Gordon & MacPhail and William
Cadenhead. All the whisky from Mannochmore goes for blending.

The advertisement '*Don't be vague: ask for Haig*' is familiar,
but less well known is the anagrammatic decomposition of
'*uisgebeatha*' – 'best: Haig, eau'. This was revealed by Dr D. G.
Altman in the *British Medical Journal* (24-31 December 1983, p.
1915). His paper on 'How Blind were the Volunteers' was part
of the riposte to Professor Dudley's 'Can Malt Whisky be
discriminated from Blended Whisky' which is referred to in the
preface, and elsewhere, in this book.

John Dewar

John Dewar, the founder of the firm, was born in 1806 and died
in 1880. He began as a wine and spirit merchant in the High
Street of Perth in 1846 when he was already middle-aged;
indeed he was over fifty before he engaged his first traveller.

The story of the rise of the House of Dewar is one of slow but sure progression.

At first in 1887 a distillery was rented at Tullymet in southern Perthshire, but in 1898 was replaced by a new distillery at Aberfeldy on the river Tay. By 1923 the firm owned seven distilleries: Aberfeldy; Lochnagar; Muir of Ord in Ross-shire; Pulteney in Wick; Aultmore, Parkmore and Benrinnes in Banffshire.

Today Dewar's can be described as a first-class blend with no special characteristics, very like Black & White or Johnnie Walker. Dewar's whisky is, after Johnnie Walker and J & B Rare, the most popular in the world and is 90 per cent exported. It never varies because it is based on many matured malts. It was fortunate to get on the market at the right time and in the right way, for it was the first whisky to be sold by the bottle. Prior to this, those wishing to take whisky home took their own jars to a hotel which had a barrel. Until Gladstone's Spirit Act of 1860 whisky could not be imported into England in bottles. The requirement to purchase it in 80-gallon casks was a great disadvantage. Success was achieved rapidly by Dewar's, for the sons of the original John were men of outstanding ability, not only in business, but in the world of affairs.

John Alexander Dewar became Treasurer of the City of Perth and for six years was Lord Provost; he also found time to become a Liberal Member of Parliament for Inverness-shire. As such he was a leader in Scottish affairs and was chairman of two Royal Commissions. In 1907 he was made a baronet and in 1917 raised to the peerage for his services. He became Baron Forteviot of Dupplin in Perthshire – the first of the whisky barons.

Thomas R. Dewar, the younger brother, was even more dynamic and was the super-salesman of the firm, travelling far and wide, and was probably more responsible than anyone else for the success of Scotch whisky in London. He began Dewar's wharf on the Thames where additional bottling was done. It was here on the old Shot Tower that Dewar's Highlander with a waggling kilt in lights used to advertise the whisky. He became a Sheriff of the City of London and sat as a Conservative Member of Parliament for St George's in the East. Knighted in 1902, he became a baronet in 1917 and in 1919 Baron Dewar of Homestall in Sussex. Three times he was Master of the Worshipful Company of Distillers, and was a great personality and wit. One of his famous sayings was 'Do right and fear no man; don't write and fear no woman.' He was a bachelor.

The House of Dewar is rightly proud of the sporting activities of the first Lord Dewar. He took a great interest in horses and dogs. He bred Cameronian which won the Derby after his death in 1930. Lord Dewar was succeeded by P. M. Dewar, who curiously enough was no relation but had worked in the office as a boy. He was Chairman from 1930 to 1946. In 1946 the third Lord Forteviot assumed control.

The company has been established in an elegant house in Haymarket, London, since 1908 and has remained there since. Dewar's joined with Buchanan in 1915 and after much deliberation became part of the Distillers Company in 1925.

The bottling and blending part at Inveralmond, just north of Perth, was opened in 1962 and strikes the eye as one comes from that direction. The rate of production is impressive and as many as 350,000 bottles can be filled in one day. Dewar's has been awarded the Queen's Award to Industry for Export Achievement on six occasions, the last being in 1984.

The blend retains its high quality and a 12 years old de luxe whisky called Ancestor is also produced. The company has the licence for Ord Distillery which is near Dingwall, north of Inverness. The single malt is now bottled as Glenordie at 12 years old. All the whisky from the original distillery at Aberfeldy goes for blending.

JOHN WALKER

The original John Walker began in Kilmarnock, Ayrshire, as a licensed grocer. Such grocers used to be very common in

Scotland and provided a method by which a lady could obtain a
bottle in the bottom of her grocery basket without being seen
coming out of a bar. After various vicissitudes (the worst being
when Walker lost all his stock as a result of a flood), he slowly
but surely recovered to become a wholesaler and supplier to
ships from the great port of Glasgow.

The business expanded rapidly under his son, Alexander,
who opened a London office in 1880. At that time the Company's brands were Walker's Kilmarnock Whisky at home and
Old Highland in export markets. Alexander died in 1889 and
was succeeded by his sons George and Alexander (Alec) who
created a new brand named Johnnie Walker in two qualities:
Red Label and Black Label together with the famous slogan
'Johnnie Walker born 1820, still going strong'. The present firm
of John Walker & Sons Ltd was formed in 1923 with Sir
Alexander Walker as Chairman.

During the First World War Alec Walker and his co-director
James Stevenson showed their great administrative abilities at
the Ministry of Munitions and Walker was knighted for his
services. Stevenson went further, becoming adviser to the
Secretary of State for the Colonies and a member of innumerable Goverment Committees. He also organised the British
Empire Exhibition in 1924. He was given a baronetcy in 1917
and in 1924 a peerage, but alas, like so many great administra-
tors, he died at the early age of fifty-three. According to
Winston Churchill, 'in ten years of public service he wrote out
and consumed the whole of his exceptional strength of mind
and body'. There is no longer a Walker as an executive in the
Company.

John Walker & Sons produces more than three million
bottles of whisky a week, which is sold in more than 200
countries. The Company has received the Queen's Award to
Industry for Export Achievement on six occasions. The main
product, Red Label, is the largest selling standard blend world
wide, but owing to a pricing dispute within the European
Economic Community it was withdrawn from the home market
between 1977 and 1983. Black Label is well recognised to be a

quite exceptionally successful de luxe whisky. Swing is another premium blend and its bottle might be regarded as a gimmick. In fact, this particular shape was first introduced in the Ships' Stores trade and its purpose was to enable it to stay upright when the ship was rolling. The Company's single malts, Cardhu and Talisker, have already been described.

JAMES BUCHANAN

The story of James Buchanan and his blend Black & White is fascinating; it is one of the perseverance and energy of one man whose great personality was worthy of Samuel Smiles's famous book *Self Help*.

He began at the age of fourteen in a shipping office in Glasgow. Here he worked long hours but, soon dissatisfied with his salary, he joined his brother, a grain merchant in that city. By the age of thirty he had moved to London and acted as an agent for Charles Mackinlay & Co, whisky merchants and blenders. This was in 1879, but by 1884 he had set up his own firm of James Buchanan & Co at 61 Basinghall Street, London. His capital was small but he succeeded in obtaining stocks of whisky from his friend W. P. Lowrie in Glasgow, who was one of the first to see the importance of blending and in this vies with the Ushers.

Convalmore distillery in Dufftown was bought by Buchanan after he had built Glentauchers near Keith. Both these distilleries are now 'moth-balled'. The company also holds the distiller's licence at Dalwhinnie which can be seen from the main road north (A9) just south of Newtonmore.

With a keen sense of business and having established a blend, James Buchanan set out to sell it in a big way using all the wiles and stratagems at his command, and he had many. He seems to have had the happy knack of choosing good advertisements. In the 1880s he obtained a contract to supply whisky to the House of Commons and for some time this was prominently displayed on the label. A quotation from the *Lancet* (31 July 1897) also was featured, which read 'Our Analysis shows this to be a Remarkably Pure Spirit, and therefore well adapted for Medicinally dietetic purposes.' The original blend was in a black bottle with a white label (which said the whisky was suitable for grog or toddy). However, demand increased rapidly and as customers began to ask for 'that black and white' whisky, the name Black & White was adopted. The black and white Scottish terriers came later and did not graduate from the back of the bottle to the front until 1975.

In 1898 James Buchanan had bought the Black Swan distillery in Holborn, London, which he rebuilt. From here came loads of whisky in the handsome drays drawn by powerful horses with immaculate drivers in picturesque stage-coach uniforms. This really was an advertisement which everyone admired. Alas they have been replaced in London by motor vans, but the drays continued in Glasgow until 1984.

Buchanan stood apart from DCL for a long while, but in 1915 the company amalgamated with Dewar's and they both joined the great company in 1925.

Portraits of James Buchanan show him to have been a tall spare man of distinguished aristocratic appearance, turned out almost as a dandy in the best Victorian manner. Like the Dewars he loved horses. When his fortunes flourished he became a successful race-horse owner and twice won the Derby. In 1920 he became a baronet and in 1922 was raised to the peerage as Lord Woolavington of Lavington, but he never lost the personal touch nor his willingness to help anyone whom he thought worked really hard and was worthy of assistance. He died in 1935 at the age of eighty-six, but his company flourished.

The headquarters office is now in St James's Square, London, opposite Distillers House.

Black & White is sold in all of the world's whisky markets, except the United Kingdom, where the Buchanan Blend was relaunched in 1978. Buchanan's de luxe is marketed only in Central and South America, where it is a highly successful brand. Black & White Premium was devised to meet consumer requirements in the Far East. Its namesake has the same role in the markets of Continental Europe and is quite a different whisky. The company acts on the conviction that consumer requirements vary substantially from Continent to Continent, but only marginally between neighbouring countries.

Buchanan's celebrated its centenary in 1984 and to mark the event published a really excellent history of the company by Brian Spiller. Much of the information in this section has come from his book. Its title *The Chameleon's Eye* may be puzzling, but is derived from a Malagasy proverb:

> Be wise, like the chameleon
> Which keeps one eye on the future
> And one eye on the past.

WILLIAM SANDERSON

Vat 69 made by the House of Sanderson, is a deservedly popular blend: it is pleasantly sweet and not too smoky. William Sanderson, who lived in Quality Street, Leith, entered his father's wine and spirit business and opened new premises in Charlotte Lane in 1864. He was particularly interested in what he called 'Mixture Whisky' – a mixture of malt and grain. He appreciated the importance of using mature whisky and he recorded in his work book:

No spirit can pay better for bonding than whisky; the first outlay averaging from two shillings to three shillings a gallon is very little and the improvement by age is far superior to the trifling interest on the first cost. Nothing tends more to increase the reputation of a spirit merchant than supplying good and well matured spirit. The distiller whose outlay is large for casks will be inclined to give better terms to the merchant who will find his own casks and it is well known that whisky stored in sherry casks soon acquires a mellow softness which it does not get when put into new casks; in fact the latter if not well seasoned will impart a *woodiness* much condemned by the practised palate. In sherry casks the spirit likewise acquires a pleasing tinge of colour which is much sought for.

This was written in 1864, and how true it is today, when

whisky is sometimes used in blends long before it is mature.

William Sanderson produced a number of liqueurs (one was called Parfait Amour) and cordials such as Green Ginger Wine and Rhubarb Wine. He also made a name for his 'whisky bitters' which was highly regarded as a 'pick-me-up and appetiser'. Nonetheless, his main interest was in what we now call blended whisky and he decided to find the finest blend to carry the name of his firm. Accordingly, he produced a hundred different blends in numbered casks and asked his friends to try them. Number 69 was chosen unanimously as being the most delectable – hence Vat 69 which was introduced in 1882. Increasing success demanded a reliable supply of good grain whisky, and William Sanderson was one of the founders of the North British Distillery Company in 1885, becoming its first Managing Director (see Chapter 11). He became a director of Lochnagar distillery, having been close friends with John Begg, and in 1886 he became a part-owner, with R. H. Thompson, of Glengarioch distillery, in Meldrum. A supply of first-class malt whisky was thus assured.

William Sanderson's eldest son, William Mark, joined his father in the family business and was responsible for the presentation of Vat 69. He coined the slogan 'Quality tells' for the famous blend. This was true of the whisky, but it was also a reference to the old family house, and subsequently business premises, in Quality Street, Leith. The dark green bottle with its familiar shape is immediately recognisable and it continues to carry the wax seal stamped with the image of the Talbot Hound which is the family crest. By the early years of this century, Vat 69 was being exported to Australia, South Africa and Canada, as well as to European countries. It was taken by Sir Ernest Shackleton on his 1914 South Pole Expedition. In 1907 Sir Ernest had favoured Old Mackinlay (Chapter 11), and there seems little doubt that a supply of whisky of one sort or another was needed for those who were facing the frozen wastes of the Antarctic.

In 1935, Booth's Distilleries Ltd (well known for their gin) amalgamated with Sanderson's, but this arrangement did not last long, since in 1937 both firms became part of DCL.

Today the House of Sanderson is a wholly owned subsidiary of the Distillers Company and continues to produce Vat 69 and Vat 69 Reserve. They received the Queen's Award for Export Achievement in 1967. Sanderson's blending and bottling is done by James Buchanan at Stepps in Glasgow and they have a head office at 63 Pall Mall, London. The company no longer operates Glengarioch distillery, but Glenesk distillery was licensed to them, although it was 'moth-balled' in 1985. J. & W. Hardie, the Leith distillers and blenders, are a subsidiary of Sanderson's: they held the licence for Benromach distillery which was closed in 1983. Hardie's are the proprietors of Old Antiquary, a de luxe blend, also produced in Glasgow by Buchanan and marketed in an elegant decanter-style bottle.

WHITE HORSE

The company, Mackie & Co Distillers Ltd, was founded by James Logan Mackie in 1883. He was one of the few heads of firms who actually worked as a distiller. He was a partner with Captain Graham at Lagavulin and together they made a blend with Lagaluvin, Craigellachie and a grain whisky.

James Mackie's nephew, Peter – nicknamed 'restless Peter' – succeeded his uncle in 1890 and the name White Horse was registered in the following year. Peter was responsible for the success of White Horse. He saw the advantages of the name, which came from an ancient inn in Canongate, Edinburgh. It is said that Bonnie Prince Charlie's officers used to drink there during the 1745 rebellion. The stage coach from Edinburgh to London set out from the White Horse Inn, every Monday and Friday and in 1754 performed 'the whole journey in eight days (if God permits)'. Sir Robert Bruce Lockhart has pointed out that White Horse had a far deeper significance than a connection with an inn. A white horse was symbolic of power and victory, of purity and high ideals. Generals regarded a white horse as lucky, for example, Napoleon's 'White Marengo' and Lord Robert's white 'Voronel'. Such romantic associations were used to good effect in advertising the whisky in subsequent years.

By the outbreak of the First World War, White Horse was the drink of innumerable army messes, and the senior author could clearly remember filling Royal Army Medical Corps panniers with it to take on service in 1915.

Peter Mackie inherited Lagavulin distillery and was one of the founders of Craigellachie distillery in 1891–3 which he bought in 1916. The latter was reconstructed in 1964. It stands on a high rock just outside the town on the Dufftown road and the gleaming stills, which can be seen through large windows, are an impressive sight.

Sir Peter, as he became, has been described as 'one-third genius, one-third megalomaniac and one-third eccentric'. But if some of these qualities can be considered rather alarming, their possessor made an enormous contribution to the whisky business. He was an ardent politician on the Unionist side but nevertheless was made a baronet by Lloyd George's Coalition Government in 1920. He died in 1924 at the age of sixty-nine leaving behind him a whisky which, by his great drive and in spite of competition, he had made famous throughout the world. The White Horse of today is, however, a much less peaty whisky than some of its predecessors of thirty years ago.

The name of the company was changed to White Horse Distillers Ltd in 1924, the year of Sir Peter's death. They also introduced a screw cap to their bottles about this time and were the first firm to do so. In 1927 White Horse joined DCL to complete the amalgamation of the 'big five'.

The company now holds the licences for Lagavulin, Craigellachie and Glen Elgin. The last two are in Speyside: Glen Elgin is fairly widely available as a single malt, but Craigellachie is seen only rarely. Presumably most of their output goes for blending. There is a touch of Islay in White Horse which no doubt comes from Lagavulin. Logan de luxe, formerly Laird of Logan's, is an excellent whisky. White Horse extra fine goes exclusively to Japan.

Distillers, Blenders and Merchants

For they should sit among the saints
That make a dram like this.

ANON

The whisky industry is made up of companies of different shapes and sizes which frequently have interests in all aspects of manufacture and distribution. In this chapter, we shall look at a variety of businesses selected by reason of the importance of their contribution or because of their interesting history. Before coming to individual firms, the general scene will be broadly reviewed in order to establish the patterns of ownership.

A BASIC STRUCTURE

There has been a tendency, as in all other industries, for mergers and take-overs to produce a forest of inter-related companies so that it is not always easy to know who owns what. Large-scale operations provide the necessary money and yet allow economies to be made by amalgamations of their component parts. But sizes does not necessarily mean efficiency and in a general way big is thought to be less beautiful than it used to be. For this reason it is satisfactory that relatively small independent family companies can exist, and apparently prosper, alongside the giants.

Although it is difficult to devise any scheme into which all the pieces of the jigsaw puzzle will fit exactly, the following main groupings emerge:

United Kingdom owned and Scottish-based whisky companies, the largest of which are:

THE DISTILLERS COMPANY
THE HIGHLAND DISTILLERIES COMPANY

Distillers* is a very large organisation which owns many distilleries and subsidiary companies, most of which are concerned with Scotch whisky sales, but its other operations include gin, vodka and other drinks, as well as food and carbon dioxide.

Highland are primarily distillers, but now own Matthew Gloag and have a share in Robertson & Baxter, both of which are blenders.

The development and main activities of these two companies are outlined in this chapter.

Then there is a group of independent companies often wholly or partly family owned:

J. & G. Grant
William Grant
Macallan
Macdonald Martin
Stanley P. Morrison

Macallan has already been discussed under its single malt and so has J. & G. Grant is relation to Glenfarclas. William Grant produce Glenfiddich and Balvenie, but the company will be referred to again later in this chapter together with Macdonald Martin, and Stanley P. Morrison.

United Kingdom breweries have steadily been buying their way into the whisky business and the main companies concerned are:

WHITBREAD
GUINNESS

Whitbread bought Long John International in 1975 and their five distilleries: Strathclyde (grain), Tormore, Laphroaig, Glenugie, and Ben Nevis (now silent).

* See postscript on p.155.

Guinness took over Bell's with their five distilleries – Dufftown, Blair Athol, Inchgower, Bladnoch and Pittyvaich – in August 1985.

United Kingdom conglomerates with interests in whisky are:

ALLIED LYONS
GRAND METROPOLITAN
LONRHO
HAWKER-SIDDELEY

Allied Lyons acquired Allied Breweries with its subsidiary Wm. Teacher & Sons in 1976. Teacher's had Ardmore and Glendronach distilleries as well as considerable blending interests.

Grand Metropolitan took over International Distillers and Vintners (IDV) which was then part of Watney Mann & Truman (brewers again). This was in 1972 and the main company has many subsidiary companies involved in brewing, food, catering and hotels. IDV's Scotch whisky interests are handled by Justerini & Brooks.

Lonrho. Scottish & Universal Investments Ltd (SUITS) became part of the Lonrho group in 1979. The holding company for SUITS' whisky business is Whyte & Mackay Distillers ltd, which includes Dalmore, Fettercairn and Tomintoul distilleries.

Hawker-Siddeley. This Group includes Carlton Industries which in turn own Invergordon Distillers Ltd. The latter have themselves a number of subsidiaries dealing with blending, bottling and marketing together with six distilleries: Invergordon (grain), Bruichladdich, Deanston, Tamnavulin, Tullibardine and Ben Wyvis. In 1985 Invergordon acquired Charles Mackinlay & Co from Scottish & Newcastle Breweries (including Isle of Jura and Glenallachie distilleries).

It is difficult to know where to include the *Argyll Group plc* who have a growing presence in the United States. Their whisky interests in the UK are managed by Amalgamated Distilled Products, with whom they are merged, and this company will be discussed in more detail later.

North American companies which have an involvement in Scotch whisky are:

SEAGRAM
HIRAM WALKER
PUBLICKER INDUSTRIES INC

Seagram have certainly established themselves on Speyside and we have already seen the number of famous distilleries which they own.

Hiram Walker began by acquiring George Ballantine & Sons Ltd. Although their bid for Highland Distilleries was unsuccessful, Hiram Walker now own nine distilleries in Scotland.

The history of these two firms is interesting and relevant to the Scotch whisky industry and they will both be considered in more detail later.

Publicker Industries Inc are in the whisky business in the USA and in the 1950s introduced a new brand, Inver House. In 1965 they built their own distillery, bottling and blending plant in Scotland near Airdrie, rather than buying Scottish companies. Today Inver House Distillers Ltd market whisky and other drinks.

European companies, now owning distilleries and also involved in other aspects of the drinks business in their own countries, are:

PERNOD RICARD (France)
COINTREAU (France)
MARTINI & ROSSI (Italy)
DYC (Spain)

Pernod Ricard bought S. Campbell & Sons in 1974 and eight years later acquired William Whiteley & Son. They now own the companies running Aberlour and Edradour distilleries.

Cointreau acquired Glenturret distillery, which has already been described, in 1981.

Martini & Rossi's subsidiary, the General Beverage Corporation of Luxembourg, now owns the Macduff distillery in Banffshire which produces the single malt Glendeveron.

Destilerias y Crianza de Whisky SA (DYC) of Madrid bought Macnab Distilleries Ltd in 1973, but apparently only a little Lochside malt is shipped to Spain (Morrice, 1983).

This outline may seem somewhat sketchy, but it is intended only to convey the impression of the widespread involvement in Scotch whisky. The interweaving of company interests is complicated and constantly changing, so that what is written now may be out of date by the time it is published. Perhaps it is wise to fall back on the initials E. and O.E. which used to grace many accounts – errors and omissions excepted (and presumably apologised for). This will certainly apply to what follows.

The companies to be described will be selected in relation to their interest in whisky rather than by their size; so although we shall be including some 'giants', like the Distillers Company, the emphasis will be on the small than the large: for example Wm. Teacher rather than Allied Lyons or White & Mackay rather than Lonrho or even SUITS. Firms which can properly be described as merchants, like Berry Bros. & Rudd or Gordon & MacPhail, will be included for their involvement in whisky and for the interest of their history. It would be ludicrous to try to make any sort of 'pecking order' and it is impossible to organise them into separate categories of Distillers, Blending Houses or Merchants because most companies take part in at least two, if not all three, of these activities. Alphabetical order will be used even if it means that large companies may find they are preceded by those which they might regard as small.

AMALGAMATED DISTILLED PRODUCTS

ADP was incorporated in 1970 to acquire A. Gillies & Co (Distillers) Ltd which operated the Glen Scotia distillery in Campbeltown and other companies whose principal activities were the distillation, warehousing, blending, broking and exporting of Scotch whisky.

During the next decade ADP expanded by acquiring various companies involved in the whisky industry. In 1982, the scale of the present company's operation was transformed by the acquisition of Barton Brands Ltd. Barton's activities are principally in the USA, but also in Scotland, and are concerned with the marketing, distribution and production of Bourbon and Scotch whiskies and other alcoholic drinks. Barton (Scotland) owned the Littlemill and Loch Lomond distilleries. In 1984 ADP merged with the Argyll Group which is a UK-based company with major interests in the food and drink business and with a growing presence in the USA.

The Loch Lomond distillery was sold to Inver House in 1985 and the Glen Scotia and Littlemill distilleries are now (1985) both closed, but held on a 'care and maintenance' basis so that production could be activated at short notice. The closure was brought about because the company held considerable stocks of both malts which were sufficient to meet foreseeable needs.

ADP produce a number of blends, the most noteworthy of which are Royal Culross, an 8 years old vatted malt; Scotia Royale, a 12 years old blend; and Morton's Royal Mile, another 12 years old blend. The company also has widespread interests in the drinks business from beer to Tequila.

ARTHUR BELL & SONS

The firm of Arthur Bell & Sons of Perth was founded in the year 1825 by T. R. Sandeman, who opened a small shop near to the ancient Kirk of St John and traded as a whisky merchant. In due course he was joined by James Roy and in 1851 Arthur Bell entered the firm. By the year 1865 Arthur Bell controlled the business and in 1895, when he took into partnership his two sons, the firm became known as Arthur Bell & Sons.

Arthur Bell died in 1900 and was succeeded by his eldest son, Arthur Kinmont Bell, who became Chairman and Managing Director when the firm was registered as a limited company in 1922. A. K. Bell believed in spending money for the benefit of his native city and his most important contribution was to establish the Gannochy Trust which has done so much to improve the amenities of Perth and to look after the welfare of its older citizens. He was made a Freeman of the city two years before he died in 1940. His younger brother, Robert D. Bell, was Managing Director for a short time.

Arthur Bell & Sons had grown up at the end of the nineteenth century as small blenders who supplied local needs and who had to purchase whiskies where they could. However, they developed rapidly and began to export whisky all over the world. Although they were affected by the depression of the early 1930s, the end of Prohibition in the USA in 1933 was recognised as a time for expansion. Bell's bought Blair Athol and Dufftown-Glenlivet distilleries in 1933 and Inchgower in 1936.

In the 1970s a programme of new building was undertaken: two new bottling complexes at East Mains (Edinburgh) and at Dunfermline; the Pittyvaich-Glenlivet distillery at Dufftown; a new head office and reception centre in Perth, and a number of maturing whisky houses. In 1983, a fifth distillery, Bladnoch, was purchased from Inver House.

Mr Raymond Miquel became Chairman and Managing Director in 1972 and over the next ten years he guided the company from pre-tax profits of £3 million to profits of £35 million. He looked for extra growth in diversification and as long ago as 1975 Bell's bought Canning Town Glass, one of the four principal companies in the bottle-making industry. In an effort to break into the largest Scotch whisky market in the world Bell's acquired Wellington Importers Ltd, a firm with headquarters in New York. A further expansion in 1984 was the acquisition of the Gleneagles Hotel Group: this included, amongst other hotels, the Piccadilly in London which was refurbished at an estimated cost of £13 million. Success might seem assured. The standard blend, Bell's Extra Special, has become the leading brand in the UK market. They also market a 12 years old de luxe blend; a 20 years old Royal Vat blend; a family of bell-shaped porcelain decanters and four single malts (Blair Athol, Dufftown-Glenlivet, Inchgower and Bladnoch). The company received the Queen's Award for Export Achievement in 1983.

Bell's independence was, however, challenged in 1985 by a takeover bid from Guinness who made their case to the public under the banner: 'Bell's has lost its way. Guinness is good for Bell's.' The battle, said to be bitter and often acrimonious, was won by Guinness on 23 August 1985, when more than 65 per cent of Bell's shareholders accepted their offer. It is to be hoped that Guinness will turn Bell's into a true world-brand.

BERRY BROS. & RUDD

The family firm of Berry Bros. & Rudd Ltd of St James's Street, London, are the owners of Cutty Sark Scots whisky. This demonstrates that a successful international business such as Cutty Sark can still be run by a small private company, even in these days of massive mergers and takeovers.

Berry Bros. & Rudd have been established at 3 St James's Street since the 1690s and their elegant early eighteenth-century premises are among the oldest buildings of their kind in London. The two families still control the firm's fortunes. Anthony Berry, the sixth generation of his family is the Chairman, and John Rudd, who is responsible for Cutty Sark, is Managing Director.

The firm's involvement in overseas markets dates back to the early part of this century, when Francis Berry, who was the present Chairman's father, began to sell the firm's wines, cognacs and Scotch whiskies in the USA. He was convinced that there was an opportunity for a new high-quality blend of Scotch whisky. At a luncheon in the partners' parlour at St

James's Street in 1923 ideas for the launch of their proposed new whisky were discussed and at a suggestion from a guest that day – the well-known Scottish artist James McBey – it was decided to call the whisky Cutty Sark. The words Cutty Sark come from Robert Burns' poem 'Tam o'Shanter', and had earlier been used to name the celebrated *Cutty Sark* clipper ship (which now lies in honourable retirement at Greenwich). It was McBey who drew the illustration of the clipper and the design for the label which included the use of the description 'Scots' whisky rather than 'Scotch', the version used more frequently today. During American Prohibition, Francis Berry had as one of his customers in the Bahamas a certain Captain McCoy, who successfully built a reputation for dealing only in 'genuine goods'. This was at a time when much of the bootleg liquor on sale in the States was of highly dubious quality. Indeed, it is said that this is where the expression 'the real McCoy' comes from.

Cutty Sark was the first of the light-coloured Scotch whiskies and the success achieved by Francis Berry meant that when Prohibition was repealed in 1933 Cutty Sark already had an excellent reputation in the United States. Berry's were to build on this through their US agents, the Buckingham Corporation (now Buckingham Wile), and in the 1960s Cutty Sark was the leading Scotch whisky in the USA; its position as one of the top brands has been maintained since that time. By the early 1960s Berry's launched Cutty Sark in other parts of the world and the company won the Queen's Award for Export Achievement in 1971. Today, Cutty Sark is one of the largest-selling Scotch whiskies in the world, being a brand leader in the two largest overseas markets, the United States and Japan, and is on sale in over 130 markets.

In more recent years Berry Bros. & Rudd have produced Cutty 12 – their 12 years old blend – which has also been introduced to many worldwide markets. The company also blend and market in small volume a number of other whiskies.

HOUSE OF CAMPBELL

S. Campbell & Son began as a blending house in 1879 and their headquarters are at Kilwinning, Ayrshire. Their interests widened in 1945 when they acquired Aberlour-Glenlivet distillery. In 1974 the House of Campbell was purchased by the French company Pernod Ricard. The Edradour distillery was acquired with the purchase of William Whiteley & Co in 1982. This firm is described at the end of the chapter. Bottling is carried out at Kilwinning and there are warehousing facilities at Aberlour, Kilwinning and Airdrie.

The malts now produced are Aberlour-Glenlivet (12 years), Edradour and Glenforres (both 12 years). Their best-known blends are Clan Campbell and House of Lords which are issued at various ages. Some publicity material is issued in French, not surprisingly, and some trilingual (English, French, Spanish).

DISTILLERS COMPANY*

The Distillers Company was formed in 1877 when six Lowland grain distillers came together to protect their interests:

John Bald & Co, Carsebridge, Alloa
John Haig & Co, Cameronbridge, Fife
M. Macfarlane & Co, Port Dundas, Glasgow
Macnab Bros & Co, Glenochil, Menstrie
Robert Mowbray, Cambus, Alloa
Stewart & Co, Kirkliston, West Lothian

The nominal capital was £2 million and the headquarters were in Edinburgh. We shall see how the company has grown and now has 363,169,545 shares in issue, with a capitalisation value of £1017 million. It is a giant, but an amiable giant and the utmost courtesy has always been shown to me when visiting its offices or its distillery managers.

DCL, as it used to be called, was fortunate in being established before the great whisky slump of 1900. Before then whisky appeared to be set for a boom market. Distillers and

* See postscript on p.155.

blenders sprang up apace until production greatly exceeded demand and many of the newcomers had to go out of business. Notorious amongst these were the Pattison Brothers who had sailed high and too near the wind. When they collapsed, their magnificent warehouses in Leith were bought by DCL for little more than one-third of their cost of £60,000.

The First World War brought great alarm to the whole whisky industry because German submarines threatened supplies of food from abroad. There was a feeling that barley, if grown at all instead of wheat, should not be used for making alcohol. Indeed much barley was requisitioned and so little whisky made that there was a shortage for many years after the war had ceased. In 1915 Lloyd George, the Chancellor of the Exchequer, already unpopular for his major increase in the whisky tax of 1909, made a speech praising Russia for reducing the making of vodka and France for suppressing absinthe. Prohibition might well have been introduced, but instead the Goverment imposed a number of restrictions. For example, the minimum legal strength of bottled whisky on the home market was reduced from 75° proof (43% vol) to 70° proof (40% vol). Of much greater importance was the Immature Spirits Act of 1915 which prohibited the delivery of whisky for consumption in the UK unless it had been matured in a bonded warehouse for at least three years. There is no doubt that James Stevenson of John Walker (Chapter 11) was influential in persuading Lloyd George to support this legislation. At the time Stevenson was a senior administrator in the Ministry of Munitions and he convinced his minister (then Lloyd George) that cheap new whisky was responsible for increased drunkenness among the workers of the country. An immediate result of the Act was a rise in the price of whisky from about 4 shillings (20p) to 12s 6d (63p) a bottle. Demands made by the Ministry of Munitions absorbed the whole output of the grain whisky distilleries. In 1917 the Government closed all malt whisky distilleries in order to conserve barley for food. The shortage of whisky stocks caused by this loss of production persisted for years after the end of the war (Spiller, 1985).

In 1919 the directors of John Haig & Co Ltd accepted an offer by DCL who then aquired the whole ordinary share capital of the company. At this time W. H. Ross was the Managing Director of DCL and he became a major figure in the subsequent amalgamations which produced the modern Distillers Company.

As early as 1915 John Dewar of Perth had joined James Buchanan of London, but it was not until 1925 that there was an exchange of shares between Buchanan-Dewar, John Walker and DCL. This was recognition by the blenders that rather than build their own grain distilleries, they should merge with their main supplier, DCL. Their unrivalled knowledge of whisky blending and distribution was thus united with the greater productive capacity of the Distillers Company. Two years later they were joined by White Horse Distillers Ltd. The development of DCL could be summarised by the words of the first Lord Forteviot (the former Sir John Dewar): 'This company has been a series of amalgamations. Its birth was an amalgamation and it has gone on amalgamating ever since.' This was said in 1927 and was true up to that time, but since then DCL has acquired only a few and not 'amalgamated' with any. In the 1984 annual report, Distillers Company PLC listed 42 subsidiaries, the great majority of which are concerned with Scotch whisky sales: only a few of their companies own bottling and blending plants. The history of the main companies (Haig, Buchanan, Dewar, John Walker, White Horse and William Sanderson) was given in Chapter 11. Some of the others will be described later in this chapter.

Scottish Malt Distillers Ltd (SMD) were originally formed in 1914 when five Lowland distilleries were merged. They were joined by other malt distilleries and in 1925 SMD became a subsidiary of DCL and have been responsible for the production of malt whisky and the works control of malt distilleries within the present company since 1930. Until recent years SMD were responsible for operating 49 distilleries, but 11 were closed in 1983 and a further 10 'moth-balled' in 1985. Most whiskies they produce are used for blending but the following single malts are now available: Aultmore, Cardhu, Clynelish, Glendullan, Glen Elgin, Glenordie, Lagavulin, Linkwood, Lochnagar, Rosebank and Talisker.

Another subsidiary, *Scottish Grain Distillers Ltd*, controls the four grain distilleries now operating: Cameronbridge in Fife; Cambus in Clackmannan; Port Dundas in Glasgow; and the Caledonian in Edinburgh. The company is also concerned with the production of carbon dioxide (a by-product of fermentation) which is used for aerated waters and beer as well as for ice-creams and as a cooling agent by the Atomic Energy Authority. Thomas Borthwick (Glasgow) Ltd sells other by-products of the whisky-making process for animal feeding stuffs.

In spite of the effects of the recent recession, there seems little doubt that the successful operating of the Distillers Company had made it possible for the whisky industry as a whole to survive the setbacks caused by the First and Second World Wars and American Prohibition in the 1920s.

The Company sold their interests in plastics and chemicals (except carbon dioxide) some years ago. In 1984 the turnover in Scotch whisky was £546 million compared with £409 million in gin, vodka and other drinks, and £178 million in other interests (mainly food and carbon dioxide). It is estimated that Distillers now have 20 per cent of the UK market for whisky (about 12 million cases) and about 40 per cent of the world market. The contribution to UK exports is important and no doubt the recent acquisition of Somerset Importers will help sales in the USA.

The head office is in Edinburgh and the London office is at 20 St James's Square. This splendid Adam house was built in the 1770s for Sir Watkin Williams Wynn and has now been beautifully restored and refurbished. Its elegance makes a visit a particular pleasure.

A number of subsidiary companies will now be described briefly with the aim of illustrating various aspects of historical and contemporary importance. The list is not comprehensive because space does not allow the detail which would be necessary to deal with all aspects of the organisation. The date given after each company is not the year it was founded, but the year it was acquired by the Distillers Company.

John Begg (1916). Lochnagar distillery was leased to John Begg in 1845 and their single malt has always been a success (Chapter 3). The company then began blending their own whiskies and built up large export sales. The standard blend is John Begg Blue Cap and they also make John Begg 12 years old de luxe.

Bulloch Lade (1927). The company were formed in 1856 when Lade & Co joined the Bulloch & Co (who owned Loch Katrine distillery near Glasgow and Lossit distillery in Islay – both long since closed). In 1857 they took over Caol Ila distillery in Islay (Chapter 4). Bulloch Lade went into voluntary liquidation in 1920 and were taken over by DCL in 1927. They now market Bulloch Lade Gold Label and Old Rarity De Luxe. A vatted malt Glen Ila is largely exported to Italy.

A. & A. Crawford (1944). This is a Leith blending firm which, like Sanderson's with Vat 69, made its name by producing a good blend, Crawford's Three Star, in the 1900s. The de luxe Five Star was marketed in the 1920s and had an increasingly good reputation. The firm started in 1860 when the brothers Archibald and Aikman Crawford set up business, near Sanderson's, in Quality Street, Leith. The brothers died in 1880 and 1885 respectively and David Ireland trained their two sons who subsequently became directors.

After the First World War the business expanded and Crawford's whisky became widely known at home and abroad. Harry Crawford died in 1927 and Archie Crawford in 1937, after which W. W. Winton became the sole Director. The company had always been merchants and blenders, but after they were acquired by the Distillers Company, Benrinnes distillery was licensed to them.

The Distillers Agency (1924). DCL set up its own export department in its early days, but in 1924 this became a separate company called the Distillers Agency. By this arrangement the Agency was originally allocated Knockdhu distillery, which was the first malt distillery built by DCL in 1893. It was subsequently licensed to another subsidiary and was closed in 1983. The Agency now holds the licence for Rosebank which is a Lowland malt distillery (Chapter 4). They also now produce the well-known and popular blend King George IV, and the de luxe Highland Nectar.

D. & J. McCallum (1937). Two brothers, Duncan and John McCallum, founded this firm in 1807. Their small inn, known as the Tattie Pit, was a favourite rendezvous for the worthies of Edinburgh. Their excellent blend, Perfection, has from small beginnings made itself known throughout the world. The de luxe McCallum is distinctly peaty and particularly good. McCallum's have held the licence for Cragganmore distillery since they joined the Distillers Company.

Macdonald Greenlees Ltd (1926). The firm of Greenlees Brothers was originally established in 1871 by the brothers James and Samuel Greenlees. At first they confined their operations to Glasgow and London where they were determined to introduce a de luxe Scotch whisky, but they realised that their task was difficult because in the Victorian era Scotch whisky was hardly known in London and was not popular. They launched Old Parr which rapidly became a most popular drink with Londoners.

Word has it that the intention of the two brothers was to hand over the prosperous business to their sons. Tragically the sons were killed in the trenches of France and the two old gentlemen by this time did not have the drive or energy to maintain their home trade business. An approach was made to Sir James Calder, who agreed to acquire the company of Greenlees Brothers. He had previously acquired Alexander Macdonald of Leith and William Williams & Sons of Aber-

deen. These companies amalgamated to form Macdonald Greenlees & Williams (Distillers) Ltd and thereafter the business
was incorporated under the name of Macdonald Greenlees Ltd.
Macdonald Greenlees now sells two de luxe brands, Old
Parr 12 years old and President, as well as Sandy Mac at
standard quality and a 12 years old Highland malt, Glendullan. Two other companies are part of the Macdonald Greenlees' group: R. H. Thomson & Company (Distillers) Ltd and
James Munro & Son Ltd. However, the vast majority of the
Macdonald Greenlees' business is Old Parr and the company is
unique in the Scotch whisky industry in that virtually all its
business is conducted with de luxe quality only.

The strength of Old Parr exists mainly in Central and South
America and Asia. Old Parr is either the leading or the second
brand in Venezuela, Panama, Colombia, Trinidad, Peru and
Paraguay, and had good prospects in Mexico before this
market was closed. The economic recession throughout the
region has had a severe effect on the business in the last two
years but the brand still retains, and in some cases has increased, its market share in these territories. Old Parr is now
the leading de luxe brand in Japan and also has other strong
markets in the Far East and Australia. The company received the
Queen's Award for Export Achievement in both 1979 and 1980.

In the EEC progress has been made in France which it is
hoped will spread to other markets once distribution difficulties
have been resolved. Sales in the UK are conducted by the
company, in a number of prestige outlets in London and Edinburgh.

John McEwan (1933). This is the company which produces the
blend Abbot's Choice. The founder, John McEwan, was a
Perthshire farmer who went into the whisky trade in the 1860s.
The company was acquired by DCL in 1933. DCL bought
Linkwood distillery in the same year and assigned the licence to
McEwan.

Donald Fisher (1936). The founder of the firm, Donald Fisher, was born in Perthshire and set up business in Edinburgh in 1826. The company was bought by DCL in 1936. They are well known for their Ye Monks brands, standard and de luxe, which have a worthwhile standing in South America and the company was honoured to receive a Queen's Award for Export Achievement in 1981.

J. & G. Stewart (1917). James Stewart was a tea and wine merchant in Edinburgh towards the end of the eighteenth century when the Stuart connection had made French wines popular in Scotland. His sons, John and George, greatly enlarged the business and in particular they developed an export trade with Sweden.

James Gray, Sons & Co became a subsidiary of J. & G. Stewart in the nineteenth century. James Gray had also been a wine and spirit merchant in Edinburgh. The family business continued till 1889 when it was bought by William Menelaws who developed his activities successfully in what were then the British Colonies.

In 1917 DCL acquired J. & G. Stewart, who by this time had very large stocks of whisky, and then in their name bought *Andrew Usher & Co*. This was a very important transaction and the history of the firm of Usher needs separate consideration.

Andrew Usher founded his business in Edinburgh in 1813. He was a successful whisky merchant and we have already seen (Chapter 5) that he was one of the first blenders of malt whiskies. He was also the first selling agent for the Glenlivet whisky. After his sons joined him, the firm moved away from trading in wines and spirits and became distillers and blenders. Andrew Usher II wanted to be certain of obtaining supplies of grain whisky and was influential in establishing the North British distillery in Edinburgh with the support of William Sanderson and others.

Two of Andrew Usher's sons went into the business and became notable benefactors of Edinburgh. Andrew II gave the great Usher Hall which is used for concerts and other similar activities. John, his brother, founded the Usher Institute for Public Health and endowed the first chair in this branch of medicine in the UK.

The blends marketed by J. & G. Stewart at present are Usher's Green Stripe and the excellent Usher's Old Vatted Scotch. The firm holds the licence for Coleburn distillery.

GORDON & MACPHAIL

The family firm of high-class grocers was established in Elgin in 1895. At the outset John Urquhart joined them to look after the whisky side of their business. The Urquhart family are now the owners and, although their shop still has its grocery trade, they not only sell wines and spirits, but can claim to be the oldest established specialist bottlers of malt whiskies in Scotland.

Gordon & MacPhail stock a very large number of different Scotch whiskies: their Connoisseur's Choice (with its characterist label) includes some very rare and very old single malts: for example, Edradour 1972; Benriach 1969; Convalmore 1969 and so on. The choice is bewildering but they also have a comprehensive list of miniatures. Examples of their oldest malts are Linkwood 1938 and Mortlach 1938 which cost about £40 a bottle: others, less expensive, are Macallan 1966, Old Pulteney 1961 and Scapa 1960. Their own vatted malt is Old Elgin and they have an interesting series: Pride of Islay; Pride of the Lowlands; Pride of Orkney; and Pride of Strathspey. Their standard blends are Glen Calder and Spey Cast.

Brief mention was made of the legal action between some distillers and some bottlers in Chapter 8. The former were concerned to protect the reputation of their own whisky and allow it only to be bottled by those authorised by them. Gordon & MacPhail are involved in this case which is still *sub judice*.

WILLIAM GRANT & SONS

The story of William Grant and his sons was given in Chapter 3 when the company's single malts, Glenfiddich and Balvenie, were described. William Grant & Sons produce their own blend, which is known as Standfast by the locals in Scotland, although the actual brand name is Grant's. In 1963, the company built a new grain distillery at Girvan which brought work to an area of high unemployment in Ayrshire. Blending is done on this site. Having secured their own supply of grain whisky (just as Usher did in 1887), they added Ladyburn malt distillery nearby in 1966. Grant's centre for bottling their blends is in Paisley, where there is a capacity to produce for sale over 2 million cases of whisky a year. A new office block was opened there in 1978.

As well as their standard blend, in its distinctive triangular bottle, there are also Grant's Royal and Grant's 12, both 12 years old de luxe blends.

The company operates a very efficient worldwide organisation, and remains the largest privately owned, independent, family whisky business. They have shown a remarkable ability to adapt to modern techniques of marketing, particularly in the 186 different countries where their whisky is sold. Their peak annual production has been equivalent to 12,900 cartons (each containing one dozen 75cl bottles at 43% vol) and in recent years they have distilled 12 per cent of the total production of Scotch whisky.

HIGHLAND DISTILLERIES

In 1887 the owners of Bunnahabhain distillery amalgamated with Glenrothes distillery to form the Highland Distilleries Company. The Chairman was W. A. Robertson who had founded the firm of Robertson & Baxter in Glasgow. Subsequently Highland acquired other distilleries: Glenglassaugh (in 1892); Tamdhu (in 1898) and Highland Park (in 1935). Of the five distilleries now owned, Glenglassaugh produces malt only for blending and others have been described in Chapters 3 and 4. In 1965 the company built a new warehouse at Buckly, near Bishopsgate, Lanarkshire.

Robertson & Baxter Ltd (R. & B.) in 1857 were whisky blenders, and wine and spirit merchants in Glasgow. In 1948 Highland Distilleries bought shares in Robertson & Baxter and now have a 35.4 per cent holding. They also have rather a complicated arrangement with Berry Bros. & Rudd and blend the famous Cutty Sark for them (Morrice, 1983). In 1965 R. & B. acquired Lang Brothers who had owned Glengoyne distillery since 1876. As well as a single malt, Lang's also produce one standard and two de luxe blends.

Matthew Gloag & Son were bought by Highland Distilleries in 1970. The original firm had begun in modern premises in Perth in 1800 and went from father to son over five generations with increasing success. Their main product was the blend Famous Grouse which is a delicious slightly peaty whisky and has justifiably become popular. Matthew Gloag were awarded the Royal Warrant in 1984. The firm's brochure used to contain a good boost for Scotch whisky:

Scotsmen the world over use it, neat to warm them when cold, diluted to refresh them when warm, to revive them when exhausted, as a medicine in sickness, as an aid to digestion, as a sedative for sleeplessness, and, universally, to celebrate the meeting with, or parting with, friends, confident that, used in moderation, it will suit the occasion as nothing else will do, and with nothing but good effect. Millions of men in every clime have found that these Scotsmen are right.

The whisky, like the sentence, is a good mouthful.

Highland Distilleries have recently made good profits and if they continue to do so will fully justify the rejection of the Hiram Walker bid in 1979/80.

INTERNATIONAL DISTILLERS & VINTNERS

IDV was founded in 1962 and their main companies are Croft & Co (established 1678); Morgan Furze & Co (est. 1715); Justerini & Brooks (est. 1749); W. & A. Gilbey (est. 1857) and Twiss & Browning & Hallowes (est. 1926). In 1972 IDV became part of Grand Metropolitan. There are now many trading arms with interests in wine and spirits other than whiskies.

IDV has three distilleries (Knockando, Strathmill and Glen Spey) which came to them through W. & A. Gilbey. A new distillery was built in 1974 at Auchroisk. Knockando produces a single malt (Chapter 3) and is managed by Justerini & Brooks. Whisky from the other three distilleries goes for blending only and this is carried out at Blythswood near Paisley. This complex was finished in 1972 and comprises seven warehouses and a process building (which includes receiving and blending tanks, filling installations and cooperage). Bulk transport of whisky was pioneered by W. & A. Gilbey in the early 1950s and a fleet of seven road tankers and one rail tanker now operate from Blythswood.

Justerini & Brooks manage IDV's distilleries and are responsible for the strikingly successful J & B Rare. The firm is one of the oldest established wine merchants in London and has had the Royal Warrant for nine successive reigns. It was established by a love-sick Italian, Giacomo Justerini of Bologna, who followed an opera singer, Signorina Belloni, to London in 1749. He brought with him the jealously guarded recipes of his uncle – a distiller from Bologna – for the making of remarkably palatable liqueurs. Fortunately he met George Johnson, who was prepared to finance the setting up of premises in Pall Mall. Justerini made up the recipes and carried out the distilling. Johnson was responsible for the office; sadly, he was killed when a runaway horse overturned his sedan chair and his son preferred to sell his share of the business. It was bought in 1831 by a Mr Brooks, a gentleman of fashion. Thus began Justerini & Brooks, who have gone from strength to strength.

J & B Rare is shipped from Scotland to 156 different countries, and today is the brand leader in the USA. The Paddington Corporation has represented J & B in the USA since 1936 and works through a network of distributors in all the States. The whisky is pale in colour and light in quality and is popular with Americans. The malts used are said to be around 7 years old. Royal Ages is J & B's de luxe whisky and is bottled at 49% vol.

INVERGORDON DISTILLERS

The Invergordon distillery, the first development of this group, is on a delightful site overlooking the Cromarty Firth, one of the great homes of the British Fleet in time of war. After the Second World War, under the inspiration of Provost Grigor of Inverness, a distillery was erected to give employment to men who had become redundant. It was, however, no ordinary distillery, but a large factory capable of making annually 10 million gallons of grain whisky by the patent still method. The first manager, Frank Thomson, a local accountant, had already enlisted the financial support of London Merchant Securities which saw the future of the project. A malt whisky distillery known as Ben Wyvis was added on the same site. Another new distillery, Tamnavulin, was constructed in 1966 in the famous Glenlivet valley and here it must be said that this new concrete building looks strangely out of place in such a Highland scene. No doubt it will, like its famous and inelegant neighbour, The Glenlivet distillery, mellow with age – the whisky, too, will improve greatly as it matures.

Bruichladdich distillery on Islay was purchased and, later in 1972, two other distilleries – Tullibardine and Deanston. Tullibardine, in the small town of Blackford, began as a brewery, but since 1949 it has made a malt whisky with a quite outstanding almost wine-like flavour. Deanston was originally a textile mill with an ample supply of water-generated electricity made from the Teith, a tributary of the Forth.

Thus it is seen that with such a plentiful supply of grain whisky and such a variety of malts Invergordon Distillers are well placed to produce really excellent blends. Findlater's Scotch Whisky and Mar Lodge (a vatted malt) are marketed internationally by Findlater Mackie Todd & Co Ltd. Invergordon's top blend is Scots Grey de luxe whisky. The company has a number of subsidiaries, in particular Longman Distillers, who produce a number of interesting vatted malts, many of which feature strongly in the export market. R. Morrison & Co Ltd were acquired in 1984 which brought

Glayva Scotch liqueur whisky into the group.

In 1985 Invergordon acquired Charles Mackinlay & Co from Scottish & Newcastle Breweries and this included the Isle of Jura and Glenallachie distilleries.

It is said that Invergordon now 'belong' to Carlton Industries which is part of Hawker-Siddeley (Morrice, 1983): in fact Hawker-Siddeley own 76.2 per cent of Invergordon's issued shares, so although a takeover is a possibility, it seems unlikely at the present time.

INVER HOUSE DISTILLERS

It was mentioned at the beginning of this chapter that this company was a part of Publicker Industries Inc of Philadelphia and built its own distillery at Airdrie. Production began in 1965. The company's main blends are Inver House Green Plaid and Red Plaid (the latter is labelled as 8 years old). Their de luxe whisky is Pinwinnie, a 12 years old blend. Mac-Arthur's is a popular cheaper brand. Those who like very sweet liqueurs, such as Tia Maria, might have a taste for Inver House Highland Cream, but I would prefer something with more whisky in it. The company are planning to introduce a new brand, Blairmohr Malt Whisky, which will presumably be a vatted malt.

Inver House sold Bladnoch distillery to Bell's in 1983 and bought Loch Lomond distillery from ADP in 1985.

LONG JOHN INTERNATIONAL

This company had its origin in 1805 when James Seager and Williams Evans established themselves in Pimlico, London, as 'makers of gin and other delectable products'. In 1898 Sir Frederick Seager Hunt, grandson of James Seager, sold the partnership to become a public company Seager, Evans & Co Ltd.

Seager, Evans continued to expand, but they did not enter the whisky industry until 1927 when their subsidiary, Scottish

Grain Distilling Co Ltd, built the Strathclyde distillery.

The next important step, as far as whisky is concerned, came in 1936 when they took over Chaplin's of Tower Hill. Chaplin's were a wine and spirit firm who had acquired Long John whisky from Macdonald's in 1911.

Long John Macdonald had built the Ben Nevis distillery at Fort William in 1823. He was a distinguished figure of great stature and physique who was descended from John Mac-Donald, Lord of the Isles. His whisky was originally a single malt, but had become a blend sometime around 1906.

Seager, Evans bought Glenugie, Scotland's most easterly distillery in 1937 to add to their Scotch interest in Strathclyde and in the Long John blends.

When the Government allowed whisky to be made again without restriction in 1953, the industry needed to expand rapidly and there were many takeovers and mergers. Schenley Industries of New York acquired Seager, Evans in 1956. A new Lowland malt distillery, Kinclaith, was built near Strathclyde (this distillery was demolished recently) and the following year it was decided to build a new distillery at Tormore on Speyside (Chapter 3) which came on stream in 1959. A 25 per cent stake in Laphroaig distillery was bought from the Johnston family in 1962 and the whole shareholding acquired by agreement after ten years.

By 1969 the distilleries of Strathclyde, Kinclaith, Glenugie, Laphroaig and Tormore all increased production and many other interests were shed. In 1971 Seager, Evans changed its name to Long John International and the whole company was acquired by the London-based brewers, Whitbread, in 1975.

The main brands owned by the company and sold throughout the world are Long John, Black Bottle and Islay Mist blends together with Tormore and Laphroaig single malts.

The Registered Office is in London and in an elegant house which was the birthplace of Lord Palmerston. The firm was founded in the same year as the Battle of Trafalgar (1805) when Admiral Nelson defeated the French fleet. This is perpetuated in the house by a room which is a replica of Nelson's cabin in his flagship, HMS *Victory*.

MACDONALD MARTIN DISTILLERIES

The name of this company may cause some confusion if its derivation is not appreciated. Macdonald & Muir Ltd acquired James Martin & Co Ltd in the 1920s and, after other acquisitions (which included the Glenmorangie Distillery Co), they formed Macdonald Martin Distilleries as a holding company. The company, like Macallan, is under close family control. For some years growing sales of Glenmorangie (Chapter 3) have been profitable, although there is a substantial investment in maturing stocks. Their main blend is Highland Queen which sells in the UK and abroad. Muirhead's blends have the same market, but Martin's VVO sells mainly in the USA and is not available in the UK.

Macdonald & Muir was founded in Leith in 1893 by Roderick Macdonald and Alexander Muir who had been 'bred to the trade'. Business expanded rapidly and they were able to move from Kirkgate to new premises at Queen's Dock, Leith, in 1902. Today their bonded warehouses remain on this site with offices in Commercial Street. We have seen that Highland Queen is a successful blend: it is named after Mary Queen of Scots who landed at Leith when she returned from France in 1561. There is also Highland Queen Grand Reserve 15 years old. The company concentrates much of its efforts on the sale of Glenmorangie, but also produces a 12 years old single malt from its Glen Moray distillery.

CHARLES MACKINLAY & CO

The first Charles Mackinlay set up business in Leith as a whisky merchant in 1815, but it was more than thirty-five years before he felt he knew his craft well enough to produce his own first new blend. His son, James, was successful in selling whisky in London and he secured a regular order for the House of Commons. In 1907 Sir Ernest Shackleton asked them to supply the whisky for his expedition to the South Pole.

Five generations of the Mackinlay family have been in the business, but in 1961 it was taken over by Scottish & Newcastle Breweries and became the Scotch Whisky division of the Waverley Group. In 1985, Mackinlay's was bought by Invergordon Distillers for £17.5 million. MacDonald Mackinlay, who is the present Chairman and Master Blender, is the great-great-grandson of the founder.

James Mackinlay, Charles Mackinlay's son, built Glen Mohr distillery with John Birnie in 1892 and later acquired nearby Glen Albyn. Both these distilleries were transferred to SMD in 1972 and were closed in 1983. Mackinlay's operated two malt distilleries for Waverley: Isle of Jura and Glenallachie on Speyside. Both were designed by Delmé Evans and were built in 1963 and 1967 respectively. Most of their whisky goes for blending, but they also have single malts on the market.

Mackinlay's Finest Old Scotch Whisky is no longer produced for the UK market, but continues to be exported to over 90 countries throughout the world. The company's premium blend, The Original Mackinlay, was reintroduced to the UK in 1985: it is based on the blend produced by the first Charles Mackinlay. It is matured in oak casks for longer than usual – and very good it is too.

STANLEY P. MORRISON

This is a relatively recently formed company which has expanded greatly during the past fifteen years. Stanley P. Morrison was a highly respected whisky broker in Glasgow and in 1951 he formed a limited company with James Howat. Morrison died in 1971 and two of his sons are now directors of the company.

Bowmore distillery (Chapter 4) was bought in 1963 and Glengarioch (Chapter 3) in 1970. The most recent acquisition was Auchentoshan (Chapter 4) from Eadie Cairns. This provides a very good spread of malts (Islay, Highland and Lowland) for blending and each is sold as a single malt. Their own brands are Old Highland and Rob Roy.

The company has interests in all facets of whisky making, and it is encouraging to see that such a successful and progressive organisation can still remain an independent family business.

NORTH BRITISH DISTILLERY COMPANY

In the 1880s, those blenders who were not part of the Distillers Company decided to build their own grain distillery in order to ensure a reliable source of grain whisky for themselves. It is not surprising that its first Chairman was Andrew Usher, whose firm had developed the vatting of malt whisky (Usher's Old Vatted Glenlivet – Chapter 5) and the blending of malt and grain whisky (Usher's Green Stripe – Chapter 11). The Vice-Chairman was John M. Crabbie, who was another Edinburgh blender. The first Managing Director was William Sanderson of Leith, whose own firm produced the well-known Vat 69 (Chapter 10), and who played an important part in developing the new distillery company. These men formed a very strong group which they needed to be in order to compete with the original Distillers Company. The aim of the North British (NB) Distillery Company was to 'stabilise prices and qualities, to resist oppression and safeguard its members' livelihood . . .'. The NB and DCL came together in 1905 to support the case for grain whisky which dominated the 'What is Whisky?' controversy (Chapter 7). The two companies also agreed in 1925 to ration their annual production to the total amounts ordered for the ensuing year. This arrangement was a response to a decline in whisky consumption at the time, which was related to Prohibition in the US and increasing taxation in the UK, and was continued until 1934.

The NB has remained an independent company whose shares can be held only by recognised whisky blenders and merchants. The Board of Directors have included most of the famous names in the Scotch whisky business and among the original shareholders were White Horse; Johnnie Walker; Usher; Sanderson; Mackinlay; Macdonald & Muir; Dewar; Crawford; Buchanan; and Bell. Many of these firms were taken over by DCL in later years. The NB continues to make grain whisky but has never been involved in blending.

The original distillery was built near Gorgie in Edinburgh and has expanded enormously over the years. More land was bought at Muirhall near Addiewall, West Lothian, in the 1960s and the 1970s, in order to build new warehouses. Production was influenced by various factors (such as the two World Wars), and like the rest of the whisky trade there have been ups and downs. The 250,000,000th gallon of proof whisky was distilled in 1970.

The NB celebrated its centenary in 1985 which has been commemorated in a book by Leslie Gardiner. This is a fascinating history and much of the information recorded here has been derived from it.

SEAGRAM

Samuel Bronfman built a new distillery in La Salle, a suburb of Montreal, in 1924 and two years later purchased Joseph E. Seagram & Sons Ltd of Waterloo, Canada, forming Distillers Corporation-Seagram Ltd. This later became the Seagram Company Ltd, which is the world's largest producer and marketer of distilled spirits and wines. Samuel Bronfman died in 1971 and was succeeded by his sons Edgar and Charles Bronfman.

In Scotland, the firm bought the Robert Brown Company in 1935 and began to lay down stocks of select Scotch whiskies for maturing. In 1948 Chivas Brothers of Aberdeen (founded 1841) was purchased and in 1950 Milton distillery, Keith, now called Strathisla distillery. Glen Keith distillery was constructed on the site of an old meal mill and began operations in December 1958. The following year, a former hydrogen factory in Keith was converted into bonded warehouses and in 1971 more land for warehouses was purchased at Mulben, some six miles west of Keith, with blending facilities following in Keith in 1975. A modern highly automated distillery, the Braes of Glenlivet, was built in 1973 to be followed by Allt à Bhainne in 1975. Seagram are to the forefront in using the most up-to-date techniques of whisky making. Glen Keith distillery was the first malt distillery equipped with microprocessors and new methods are tested there.

In 1964, a striking administration building, the Company's head office, was opened by Samuel Bronfman at Paisley: this site also contained bottling, warehousing and distribution services. Additional warehouse and blending facilities were obtained at Dalmuir in 1968 and even more at Balgray in 1972. Increased production requirements were met in 1981 by the construction of a bottling hall at a cost of £12 million in Paisley.

The whisky firm of The Glenlivet and Glen Grant Distilleries Ltd (including Hill Thomson & Co) was purchased in 1978; its famous distilleries of The Glenlivet, Glen Grant, Longmorn, Caperdonich and Benriach operating under the production company, Chivas Brothers Ltd.

The company's rich de luxe Chivas Regal blend is made from top well-matured malts and is marketed along with 100 Pipers, Passport, Queen Anne and the 21 years old Royal Salute blends. Their excellent single malts, The Glenlivet, Glen Grant and Strathisla have been described in Chapter 3.

Seagram still advertise 'Drink Moderately' and have as their motto 'Integrity, craftsmanship and tradition'. To this could be added 'quality first'.

STEWART & SONS OF DUNDEE

This company should not be confused with J. & G. Stewart of Edinburgh, who are part of Distillers Company.

The Dundee firm was founded in 1831 and was one of the many Scottish companies which took advantage of the newly invented Coffey still and the demand for blended whisky. They did not own their distillery and were not at the time part of any whisky combine. Thus they avoided the restriction of 'economic demands inseparable from the ownership of distilleries'. Stewart succeeded in making a flavoursome and above-average blend, Cream of the Barley, for which there was such a large demand that they had greatly to increase their bottling and blending facilities in 1967. Their de luxe blend is now Royal Stewart 12 years old.

Stewart's of Dundee became part of Allied Breweries in 1969 and their business was increased by the purchase of the Curtis Distillery Company since then. The current blend Curtis de luxe (5 years old) is much better than the original Scotsman's Head, which the senior author remembered from the late 1930s. It is a typical light blend with no disagreeable features and the 12 years old is better still.

WILLIAM TEACHER

This is another company which is part of Allied Breweries, having been taken over in 1976. Allied Breweries itself has been part of Allied-Lyons since 1981.

William Teacher must have been a determined young man to have founded his Glasgow firm in 1830 when he was only nineteen years old. By the time he was forty, he had established eighteen Teacher's Dram Shops at which customers could drink on the premises. As business expanded a new head office was opened in Argyll Street, Glasgow, in the early 1850s and this was where the company's wholesale business started. Although William died at the comparatively early age of sixty-five, he was a patriarchal figure during the later part of his life; a tall man with a flowing beard who was a strict Victorian in the conduct of his business and his family. Insobriety and smoking were not allowed. His eldest son, also William, took charge but died four years later in 1880 at the age of forty-three. The second son, Adam, found himself at the head of a rapidly growing enterprise. The first William's grandson, William Curtis, was brought into the business when he was seventeen.

The blend Highland Cream, on which the company now

concentrates, was first registered in 1884 and the great success which it has had reflects well on the skill of the founder and his successors. Work on building Ardmore distillery was started in 1897, but a year later Adam died. The firm encountered considerable financial problems which came at a very bad time for the whisky industry generally – this was when the Pattison crash occurred. However, Teacher's survived, probably because they had strengths not enjoyed by many others: the retail shops, the bottled whisky trade, the sales of bulk blended whisky and the developing export business.

Teacher's remained a purely family business for three generations, but a private limited company was formed in 1923 which became a public company in 1949. Although there are no longer any Teachers, the family is represented by descendants through the female line.

In 1955 production at Ardmore was doubled and the office at Enoch Square was expanded a year later. Glendronach distillery (Chapter 3) was bought in 1960 and it was in this year that Teacher's sold the last of their retail shops in Glasgow. New blending and bottling facilities at Craigpark were brought into operation in 1962.

In the late 1960s Teacher's introduced a new bottle for their Highland Cream with a 'gold' jigger cap. The company has obviously always been interested in how best to close and open their bottles because in 1913 William Bergius (the son of the original William's daughter) produced a new device to replace the standard cork. The new design was called the 'self-opening bottle' and was coupled with the advice to 'bury the corkscrew'.

Highland Cream is of excellent quality with a pleasant sweet flavour, but slightly more peaty than Vat 69. It is the second best-selling brand in the UK and is exported worldwide through Teacher's distribution network. There is, for example, a wholly-owned subsidiary in Brazil who bottle bulk exports. The company has more international links than any other member of the Allied-Lyons group. The de luxe Royal Highland whisky all goes for export. The single malt Glendronach is bottled at 8 and 12 years (40% vol).

HIRAM WALKER

In 1930 Hiram Walker-Gooderham & Worts Ltd of Canada made its first venture into the Scotch whisky trade by acquiring a 60 per cent interest in the Stirling Bonding Company and J. & G. Stodart. The remaining shares in these companies were obtained in 1936. In the same year the company extended its blending interests by the acquisition of George Ballantine & Son Ltd. They also entered the field of the production of Scotch whisky with the acquisition of two Highland malt distilleries: Glenburgie and Miltonduff. The company experienced difficulty in obtaining sufficient quantities of grain whisky to meet its estimated requirements and the decision was taken to build Dumbarton grain distillery as well as Inverleven malt distillery which went into production in 1938. In 1937 Hiram Walker & Sons (Scotland) Ltd was formed and became the parent company of the group in Scotland.

Distilling was suspended during most of the Second World War, but exports of blended whisky continued throughout this period. When production was resumed in 1946 two further warehouses were built at Dumbarton to house the stocks of maturing whiskies and a bottling facility was installed.

In 1951 a firm of maltsters, Robert Kilgour of Kirkcaldy, was acquired to provide a source of malt for the group's distilleries. The maltings at Kirkcaldy were subsequently modernised and enlarged.

During the 1950s the group's export trade expanded rapidly, and in order to obtain the necessary stocks of maturing whiskies to service its projected export sales, it acquired a number of companies holding stocks of maturing whiskies and a further three Highland malt distilleries: Glencadam, Scapa and Pulteney (Chapter 3). Since the 1930s two further malt distilleries have been acquired: Balblair in 1969 and Ardbeg in 1976 (Chapter 4).

The company received the Queen's Award for Export Achievement in 1968 'for their industrial efficiency as manifest in the furtherance and increase in Export Trade'.

The growth in export sales over the years resulted in the production facilities at Dumbarton becoming inadequate to deal with the volume of whisky to be stored, blended and bottled. In the 1950s and 1960s a 65-acre complex of whisky warehouses was constructed at Dumbuck just outside Dumbarton, and a further maturation complex has been built on a 200-acre site at Beith. At the Dumbuck warehouses a unique flock of geese – known as the 'Scotch Watch' – keep a constant vigil over the millions of gallons of whisky lying maturing. This is reminiscent of the geese on Capitol Hill in Ancient Rome which gave warning of marauding Goths. A further site at Kilmalid, Dumbarton, was more recently acquired and a blending facility costing £7 million was constructed which went into production in 1977. In 1983 a bottling facility was also built at Kilmalid with a potential capacity for bottling 88 million bottles per year.

The company does not market any Scotch whiskies under its own name, but their major brands are Ballantine's; Old Smuggler and Ambassador. They also produce many other brands such as Lauder's; Marchant's; King's Choice; Mackintosh; Old Original; Grand Macnish; and Doctors' Special.

WILLIAM WHITELEY

Although his grandfather began the business in Leith, it was William Whiteley (1856–1941) who founded the company in 1922. He spent his lifetime in whisky and became the doyen of the Leith blenders. His company was bought by an American in 1938. Another American financier bought it in 1978 and ran it under the name of J. G. Turney & Co. The most recent change was in 1982 when the House of Campbell, a subsidiary of Pernod Ricard, purchased the business. In spite of these financial exchanges William Whiteley still continues as an active company with a very large number of brands of whisky selling worldwide and particularly in the USA. The best known in the UK are House of Lords and King's Ransom.

William Whiteley purchased Edradour (sometimes called

Glenforres) distillery in 1933 and continues to hold the licence. This is in many ways Scotland's most picturesque distillery and is situated in the hills on the east of Pitlochry at Balnauld. It was founded in 1837 on one side of a burn with steep banks. It is small and the spirit still holds only about 300 gallons (1300–1400 litres). One man on each shift can handle all the production of the distillery. Although the company has never bottled Edradour as a single malt, it is available in Gordon & MacPhail's Connoisseur's Choice. Glenforres, 12 years old, is a vatted malt.

WHYTE & MACKAY

James Whyte was manager of Allan & Poynter who had a bonding business which is recorded in the *Glasgow Directory* of 1844. In 1882 James Whyte went into partnership with Charles Mackay. The new firm grew steadily and their success was based on original advertising and active promotion of their Special blend. They introduced an original shaped bottle with a measure cap rather similar to Teacher's. Their whisky was sold throughout the world, the principal markets at first being the USA, Canada and South Africa.

A merger with Dalmore distillery in 1960 resulted in a new company called Dalmore, Whyte & Mackay. In 1972 they joined Sir Hugh Fraser's Scottish & Universal Investments Ltd and with this financial backing were able to add two Highland malt distilleries to the group: Fettercairn (Chapter 3) and Tomintoul. Tomintoul is the highest distillery in Scotland and was built in 1964–5.

The next development took place in 1979 when Whyte & Mackay became part of Lonrho – an international conglomerate with widespread interests.

Whyte & Mackays' Special is a whisky with a light flavour to suit modern taste. The process of 'double marriage' perfected by their Master Blender is considered the key to its quality. The matured malt whiskies are blended and married for six months; then the malt and grain are brought together and the blend is put back in the cask to mature further. There are two other high-class blends: de luxe and 21 years old. Dalmore, Old Fettercairn and Tomintoul are available as single malts. The last named is in a very fancy bottle which is not without its critics. The company have maintained their reputation for innovative packaging: for example, a pot-still decanter, a double tantalus for their de luxe whiskies and a cut-glass decanter for the special Harrods 21 years old whisky. Also useful for presents is the Scotch whisky collection (miniatures of their three malts and three blends) and the Highland Malt pack (½-litre bottles of Dalmore and Fettercairn).

POSTSCRIPT (*10 April 1987*)

DISTILLERS COMPANY PLC. In spite of its huge size and its past successes, the company became a candidate for a take-over bid because of 'its inability to adapt to a rapidly changing alcohol market' (*The Times*, 2 Sept. 1985). The Argyll Group made an offer of £1.9 billion in December 1985 and an acrimonious battle ensued. Distillers claimed that they had re-organised their structure over the past two years, and their new Chairman appeared to be confident that the company could weather the storm. The situation was difficult, but Distillers welcomed a counter-offer of £2.2 billion from Guinness in an agreed take-over bid. Litigation on various points followed. Guinness made a second bid of £2.46 billion which was not referred to the Monopolies and Mergers Commission since they had made a firm commitment to sell seven of the Distillers' brands (including Haig and Claymore) to Lonrho's Whyte & Mackay for £10.5 million. Argyll raised their bid to £2.8 billion, but on 18 April 1986 Guinness, now with an equal bid, announced that they had obtained just over 50 per cent of Distillers' shares; and so their take-over was successful. Distillers' troubles were still not over, as revelations from the Boesky affair in New York cast doubt on Guinness' financial manipulations during the take-over. Their Chairman, Mr Ernest Saunders, was obliged to resign and was replaced by Sir Norman Macfarlane.

12

The Pleasures of Whisky

*Whisky, properly savoured and not grossly gulped,
is essentially a pensive and philosophic liquor.*
IVOR BROWN, *Summer in Scotland*, 1952

We drink to quench our thirst, to enjoy the taste as it goes down and to experience the pleasurable sense of well-being and relàxation which a moderate amount of alcohol produces. Whisky is not in itself an especially good thirst quencher, so that this chapter will be mainly about the smell and taste and how best to appreciate it. In conclusion a review of the past and present attitudes of doctors to drink will allow a brief survey of the effects of alcohol.

THE TASTE

It should be possible to persuade the reader, by a well-worded description of the taste of a particular whisky, that he would gain exceptional enjoyment from it. This might be a mistake because the gustatory experiences of a whisky expert might well not be matched by those of an inexperienced whisky drinker. There are some unfortunate people who dislike the taste and it could be difficult to convince them otherwise. Those who are prepared to learn will do well to take their whisky drinking seriously and so obtain the most pleasure from it.

David Daiches (1983) writes that 'the taste of a good Scotch whisky is so subtly compounded of bouquet, the actual taste of the palate, the after-taste . . . that one man's account of his experience in drinking a given whisky may be very different from that of another who enjoys it equally.' This expresses the difficulties of communicable description, but immediately gives you the three aspects (bouquet, actual taste and after-taste) to think about when you drink a good whisky. By doing this it becomes easier to compare subtleties of different whiskies. But what words to use for description? As with wine (and, for all I know, tea) there is a special vocabulary used by experts which often confounds the ordinary person. Let us take a look at a number of descriptive terms used by the tasting panel in the 1985 edition of *Harrods Book of Whiskies*:

– 'still-house aroma'
– 'touch of the spice cupboard'
– 'hot dry hardness in the after-taste'
– 'peaty, slatey, medicinal, iodine, ozone, even fish boxes'
– 'an intense explosion of flavour'
– 'slightly rubbery nose'

Some of these expressions may seem somewhat far-fetched, but they are a genuine attempt to characterise aroma and flavour in order to convey olfactory and gustatory sensations to the reader. An element of 'connoisseurmanship' is present which is entertaining and in no way objectionable. But the best thing is to try and see.

THE CHOICE

The large number of malts and the much larger number of blends can leave the drinker bewildered before he starts (let alone afterwards). To some extent the choice depends on what can be afforded and how and when it is to be drunk. People often want to know 'What is the best whisky?', but this is no more sensible than asking 'What is the best wine?' Comparisons cannot be made between sauterne and claret, any more than between a malt (like Glenmorangie) and a blend (like Bell's).

For the thirsty, who are going to add double the volume of water, and even ice, any of the standard blends are excellent at

£8 to £9 a bottle. If you like what you know, it may be best to stick with it, but a little experimentation with unknown brands is worthwhile.

The de luxe blends were discussed briefly in Chapter 9 and cost from £12 a bottle upwards, which is about the same price as a single malt, and here there is plenty of scope for trial. It may be best to start with one of the most popular single malts, such as Glenfiddich or Glenmorangie, and then branch out to Islay and the Lowlands. Earlier chapters (3 and 4) give guidance which should help with the choice. Miniature bottles (5cl) are an excellent way of discovering inevitable likes and dislikes without too much expense. They are available in Scotland as we have seen, but good selections are not so easy to find in England. Those who collect miniatures recommend D. M. & D. Shaw, Bolton Street, Blackpool; Seabourne Wines, 173 Seabourne Road, Bournemouth; and The Whisky Shop, Bailgate, Lincoln.

Finding a bottle (standard size) of what may prove to be a favourite malt in England is certainly not as difficult as it was. Many supermarkets stock a variable number, but sometimes these are relatively expensive in such places to offset a reduction in cost of a cheaper 'own' brand. It is best to find a good local wine and spirit merchant and ask for his help. If London is accessible, Harrods has about 46 different single malts on their list, and Fortnum & Mason 38. The mecca in London is still Milroy's Soho Wine Market, 3 Greek Street, where about 93 varieties are available. Otherwise it might even be necessary to go to Scotland. An interesting source is the recently formed *Scotch Malt Whisky Society* whose headquarters are 87 Giles Street, Leith, Edinburgh. The Society began as a syndicate of friends 'who got together to buy whisky in the cask because they believed it tasted better straight from the wood'. This avoids the process of 'chill-filtering' as was discussed in Chapter 8. Members are able to buy bottles of the specially chosen malts which are identified obliquely by clues given in the quarterly newsletter. This is not too difficult, particularly for those who do crosswords. These are strong whiskies, certainly not diluted with tapwater and usually with strengths from 56% vol to 64% vol. They are to be recommended to the aficionado with £16 to £20 to spend.

WHEN TO DRINK IT

A Highland farmer, who had to face a wet dark morning, would invariably start the day with a dram to get himself going and to keep out the cold. Dr Johnson denied tasting whisky when he travelled to the Western Isles in 1773, but he did however observe, apparently without surprise, that 'a man of the Hebrides . . . as soon as he appears in the morning, swallows a glass of whisky'. He went on 'yet they are not a drunken race . . . but no man is so abstemious as to refuse the morning dram, which they call a skalk'.

Times have changed and most people confine their whisky drinking to the hours after six o'clock in the evening. As an aperitif a good dry blend or malt is excellent. A long 'thin' whisky and water, with or without ice, is appropriate for the hot and thirsty. After dinner a well-matured rich whisky, like Glenlivet or The Macallan, can be savoured in a brandy glass. Haggis is not often eaten by other than Scots, but anyone faced with it will find that it goes down well when accompanied by neat whisky of any kind.

So whisky in its many forms can be regarded as a universal drink and the one to take to a desert island (bought, of course, in the duty-free shop before you go).

WATER?

There are those who feel that a good malt whisky should not be adulterated with any water at all, and they will have the support of such connoisseurs as David Daiches. Others, for example Wallace Milroy, will say that just a dash of water brings out the aroma and the flavour. Certainly no one is going to be right in this argument, because many (and I used to be one of them) like their whisky diluted half and half. The Scotch Malt Whisky Society seems to support this school suggesting that it is what the distillery workers on Speyside do. Of course, stronger whiskies need to be diluted even more. At, say, 60% vol three or even four parts of water should be added. Dilution is certainly economical and makes an expensive whisky go much further, so relatively it is not more expensive at all. But overdilution can definitely take away some of the best taste and I really think that I would now sit on the fence and say that a good malt (at 40% vol) should be drunk with half as much water as whisky.

Having come to this conclusion, I read for other reasons my copy of Kingsley Amis's *On Drink* (1972) and was interested to find that he was of the opinion that 'dilution with just less than an equal part of water is the point at which all the alcohol will enter your bloodstream – a fact, known without the benefits of science, to Scotch and Irish drinkers for two centuries'. He suggests, in fact, that if you want to drink less you should 'try drinking neat un-iced spirits, a practice so gruelling that . . . actual intake is almost bound to drop. . . .'

There is finally the rather special method of 'shoogling'. This we have seen in Chapter 3 was the way Ned Shaw, who was the manager of Inchgower distillery, said 'the great drinkers in my time took their whisky. They'd take a dram of whisky first and then some water, and *shoogle* the mixture around in their mouth' (quoted by Jack House in *Pride of Perth*).

The next question is, what water? Tap water is often heavily chlorinated and this will spoil the taste of a good whisky. Filter jugs can be bought which help, but nowadays mineral water is readily available in bottles: Highland Spring water or still Malvern water are best. The cost is negligible compared to the price of whisky.

FOR BEGINNERS

Since good whisky is to be enjoyed and savoured, some consideration should be given to the drinking vessel. The glass should be solid and heavy in the hand, but comfortable to hold. It should be of sufficient size to allow the whisky to be swirled around in it. This manoeuvre (and warmth from the hands) releases the aroma and blenders, who are not drinking, use a glass like a sherry copita for their nosing, and they do swirl it around vigorously. The glass designed for the competition held by the Bowmore distillery (Chapter 4) was broader than the traditional kind. One of the criteria which the judges were looking for was that the glass should be 'distinctive and recognisable, ideally as instantly identifiable with malt whisky as the balloon shape is with brandy'. Rosa Brandon's winning entry achieves this. Most drinkers, however, prefer an ordinary short stout tumbler. It should be sufficiently large, about 150-200 cl, to allow the whisky to be swirled without spilling. Edinburgh crystal is excellent.

There really is no need to be confused by the foregoing discussion and what the tiro should do is quite simple. First, as Mrs Beeton has it, you must catch your hare: that is buy good malt whisky, a bottle of water (preferably) and your most suitable glass. A modest amount, say 3 or 4 cl, should be poured: a larger size tumbler is used, not to be filled, but to allow the whisky to be agitated. This should be done and the aroma appreciated – perhaps after warming between the hands. Then it should be sipped, neat. Add a splash of water and try again. Then dilute it progressively (you may now have to try another dram) and decide which way you like it best. There is no need to accept anyone else's dictat. I am, however, quite sure that the flavours of good whisky can be properly appreciated only if it is sipped, not gulped.

It is probably worth using the same sort of procedure with de luxe whiskies – after all they are expensive. If all this is too much fuss and trouble, then a good blend with water can be gulped and enjoyed in a different way: a very good cocktail party drink. Cheaper supermarket brands may be chosen by some but it is important to be sure that the bottle contains 75 cl (not 70 cl) and the strength is 40% vol – otherwise it should be labelled 'under strength'. It may not be the bargain it seems.

Finally, and it should scarcely be necessary to add this, *never* add soda water to a malt. I have found, when I have done it by mistake, that soda seems to do something dreadful to a malt, making it almost undrinkable.

THE BEST MALT?

We have already said that the question 'What is the best whisky?' is unanswerable, but if the beginner needs guidance about which malt to start with, the tasting test organised by the *Sunday Times* in 1975 gives an indication of the field to be considered. A panel, which included the senior author, met and tasted 20 different malts from Milroy's selection. The individual scores were combined to form an 'excellence quotient' and the first five top scorers were:

The Macallan	1963	42% vol
Tormore	10 years	43% vol
Glen Elgin	12 years	43% vol
Bowmore	12 years	40% vol
The Glenlivet	12 years	40% vol

The next six were: Aberlour, Glenfiddich, Glengoyne, Inchgower, Laphroaig and Rosebank. Taste varies and another panel might well have chosen differently, but this is a wide selection any one of which is likely to be enjoyed by most people. Other distinguished malts have not been mentioned here but the descriptions of them are given in Chapters 3 or 4.

TASTING TESTS

The results of the *Which?* tests which were described in Chapter 9 seem to throw a damper over the niceties of blended whisky. The panels of Scottish men and women failed to distinguish between standard blends and de luxe whisky on the first occasion, and between standard and the 'cheaper' blends on the second. The exact methods of random tasting and the statistical analysis of the results (and their significance) was not revealed, so the critical whisky drinker might be sceptical.

A rather more disturbing and disappointing trial comes from Professor Dudley's Surgical Unit at St Mary's Hospital, London. This was published in the *British Medical Journal* (24-31 December 1983) in a paper entitled 'Can Malt Whisky be discriminated from Blended Whisky? The Proof. A Modification of Sir Ronald Fisher's hypothetical tea-tasting experiment'. Perhaps it should be said at this point (and it might be guessed from the title) than the *British Medical Journal* changes its spots a little at Christmas, publishing some interesting and amusing articles which occasionally can be regarded as nothing other than spoofs. This is not to say that the whisky tasting was not serious. But peer commentaries were also published. Sir James Howie's was called 'Good motivation but indifferent methods' and criticised the choice of malts and blends which were used in the experiment. Dr Altman, in his paper 'How blind were the volunteers', raised doubts about the statistical methods. So it is necessary to take the conclusion of the trial with some caution: this was that malt whisky could not be distinguished from blended whisky and that experience did not alter the powers of discrimination. Professor Dudley's riposte – 'In defence of the whisky drinker on the Clapham omnibus' – does not entirely carry conviction: he does agree that his research should continue along the lines suggested, but a grant would be necessary to subsidise it.

The *Decanter* magazine carried out a test with malt whiskies and brandies in 1977. The seventeen tasters were mostly experts (or apparently so) and each sampled from ten numbered decanters. Five were correct for 8 out of 10; three scored 9 and five got them all right. The 'nose' was noted to be a more important distinguishing factor than taste. They concluded that 'even quite experienced drinkers can mistake malt whiskies for cognac (or vice versa)', which says something for the quality of malt whisky (or so some would think, but perhaps the reverse is true).

There is no doubt that some experts can recognise individual whiskies accurately and many informal tasting sessions have shown this to be true. It depends what is being drunk because almost no one could fail to distinguish between, say, Laphroaig and The Glenlivet.

Tasting tests are amusing and interesting, but perhaps the results should be taken with a pinch of salt (or better still, a glass of whisky).

TODDY AND ATHOLE BROSE

Whisky can be used, and sometimes misused, in many different ways, but these two traditional Scottish drinks are not to be scorned.

Toddy is simply whisky, sugar and hot water. The tumbler should be warmed and then sugar added (2 or 3 lumps). Then boiling water is poured in to half fill it, followed by an equal volume of whisky. This is strong stuff (depending on the size of the tumbler) and may help to relieve the symptoms. The warm glow which follows is induced by dilatation of the blood vessels in the skin (a physiological effect of alcohol). Maybe the blood vessels on the nose are affected too so that congestion may be increased. I suspect that resistance to the germs may be reduced so that the benign effects of the toddy may have made matters worse the next morning. However, this heresy is not science and if you need to, try it and see. But it may not be wise to follow Sir Robert Bruce Lockhart's advice which was to put one bowler hat at the foot of your bed and drink toddy till you can see two.

Athole or atholl brose comes in many forms and Scottish families often have their own special recipes. Strictly, brose is a dish made by pouring boiling water (or milk) on oatmeal (or oatcake) seasoned with salt and butter, but athole brose can be a drink, when the constituents are honey, fine oatmeal, a little water, and malt whisky. This should be stirred vigorously until it froths and then kept in a bottle for two days. The same ingredients, without the water, can be used to make the delicious pudding called Cranachan, when the oatmeal is toasted, and mixed with honey, malt whisky and whipped cream. Raspberries or blueberries can be added in season.

THE EFFECTS OF ALCOHOL

Man seems to have made and drunk alcohol, in one form or another, since time immemorial. A reason for this was most simply expressed in the Psalms: wine maketh glad the heart of man. Having considered the particular pleasures of whisky drinking, we will turn to the general effects of alcohol and why its use has given pleasure to so many people. It would certainly be idle to deny that many of those who drink whisky do so for its alcoholic effect.

Alcohol is absorbed by the stomach and quickly reaches the brain. Its immediate effect is to induce a feeling of well being and release from tension. This must be good, but what happens next varies a great deal with the individual concerned. If more and more is drunk, some become quiet and others excitable. Eventually there is a loss of control and coma, because we are, after all, taking an anaesthetic drug. Most drinkers learn how much to drink to enjoy the pleasurable effects and to avoid the severe penalties of excess.

DOCTORS AND DRINK

The medical profession has always been interested in drink, prescribing it for themselves and their patients; but nowadays many are concerned with what is called alcohol abuse.

We have already seen (p.115) that a quotation from the medical journal, the *Lancet*, was used on the labels of Buchanan's whisky to extol its virtues. This was in the last years of Queen Victoria's reign. The Edwardians, as might be expected, did rather better and the *Lancet* of 1907 provided a long pronouncement which was used by Vat 69:

In view of the statements frequently made as to present medical opinion regarding alcohol and alcoholic beverages we the undersigned think it desirable to issue the following statement, a statement which we believe represents the teaching of leading clinical teachers as well as that of the great majority of medical practitioners. Recognising that in prescribing alcohol the requirement of the individual must be the governing rule, we are convinced of the correctness of the opinion so long and generally held that *alcohol is a rapid and trustworthy restorative.* In many cases it can be truly said to be truly life-saving owing to its power to sustain cardiac and nervous energy while protecting the wasting nitrogenous tissues. As an article of diet we hold the universal belief of civilised mankind that the moderate use of alcoholic beverages is for adults usually beneficial, amply justified.

We deplore the evils arising from the use of alcoholic beverages. But it is obvious that *there is nothing however beneficial which does not in excess become injurious.*

The statement was signed by sixteen eminent men including the Professor of Medicine in Glasgow, Sir William Gowers; the famous London neurologist, Sir Thomas Fraser; Professor of Materia Medica and Clinical Medicine in Edinburgh; and the Professor of Physiology at King's College, London, who was McDowall's predecessor. Much of what they wrote can now be regarded as outdated rubbish, but their general sentiments were very proper at the time. Even today the ability of alcohol to dilate the peripheral blood vessels may be beneficial.

But something much more has happened: there is some evidence to show that those who drink alcohol may have a decreased risk of having a coronary thrombosis. Such facts as there are seem to suggest that men who drink less than one bottle, perhaps two-thirds of a bottle, of whisky a week (or an equivalent amount of any alcohol) may live longer and have fewer heart attacks than teetotallers. It has to be said, because it really seems to be true, that the limit is lower (say, half a bottle a week) for women.

The bad news has to follow. Too much alcohol does lead to cirrhosis of the liver and death. Alcoholics are liable to be overweight, but suffer from vitamin deficiency. They are likely to perform badly in intelligence tests and their brains are reduced in size. Gastritis and sickness are common and there is an increased incidence of cancer of the mouth, throat and liver. The whole problem has been well reviewed in *Which?* magazine (October 1984).

The overall consumption of alcohol has increased in the UK

and in other countries. A particularly distressing aspect is youthful drunkenness, often expressed in hooliganism at football matches. The fact of the matter is that alcohol abuse has doubled over the past twenty years. Dr Michael O'Donnell drew attention to this in a BBC television programme broadcast in April 1985. He pointed out that abuse was directly related to the general availability of alcohol and to its consumption. He also quoted recent research carried out in Lothian which showed that a modest price rise produced a fall in harmful effects among heavy drinkers. This led him to conclude regretfully that the price of reducing alcohol abuse, and its horrifying social and medical effects, is one that 'we will have to pay, or at least all of us who enjoy drinking'.

The French Government clearly acknowledges the problem and decided in 1983 to introduce a new tax called the *vignette*, to finance the increased costs of their health services produced by excessive consumption of alcohol. This was to be levelled on drinks with an alcohol content of over 25% vol, but here a certain illogicality crept in since 88 per cent of the alcohol consumed in France is French wine or beer, which do not attract the new tax. Furthermore, a large amount of state aid was given to producers in the Cognac, Armagnac and Calvados regions (*Distilling Sector Working Group Report*, 1984). Although the *vignette* was designed to raise money for health, the main sources of French alcoholism were excluded and whisky was discriminated against.

Finally it must be emphasised again that the last few paragraphs concern alcoholic drinks in general and do *not* particularly apply to whisky. 'White spirits' have become increasingly popular and white wine is fashionable in bars and at home. A popular misconception that wine is 'weaker' than whisky needs to be dispelled. The typical pub measure of white wine (at 11% vol) in a 12 cl glass contains more alcohol and more calories than a pub measure of whisky.

So if you like whisky you should drink it, but it may be worth considering paying more (for better quality) and drinking rather less, with more pleasure.

13

The Whisky Industry Today

*The operations of the Scotch whisky industry
are a good deal more complex than acquaintance
with its end product might suggest . . .*
Distilling Sector Working Group Report,
1978

SOURCES OF INFORMATION

Unravelling the complexities of the whisky industry is obviously a job for the expert, but it is possible to make some observations and note certain trends without having spent a life-time in the business. Statistics are available and their sources will be acknowledged now, rather than at the end of the chapter. Two bodies, in particular, provide important information:

The Scotch Whisky Association (SWA) was formed in 1942, taking over the functions of the previous Whisky Association. Its aims are basically to 'protect and promote the interests of the Scotch whisky trade generally, both at home and abroad'. The membership, numbering 118 in 1985, is made up of companies concerned with all aspects of the whisky business. Headquarters is in Edinburgh and there is also an impressive office at 17 Half Moon Street, London. The *Statistical Report* for 1984 is a valuable source.

The Distilling Sector Working Group (DSWG) (*Scotch Whisky*) meets under the auspices of the National Economic Development Council and has produced reports in 1978 and 1984. The sixteen members of the group are drawn from the industry, representing both management and unions, and also includes civil servants from relevant government departments or agencies. Facts or figures from their latest report will be acknowledged by the reference: *DSWG* (1984).

Much information in newspapers and journals comes from these sources, but a broad survey of Distilled Spirits by Nicholas Faith, published in *The Economist*, 22 December 1984 (NF, 1984), ranges rather further and is particularly interesting.

An appendix in the previous edition of this book (1975) was written by Dr I. A. Glen and began 'The Scotch whisky industry encounters peculiar financial problems because of the prolonged gap between the production and consumption of its product.' This reflects the time needed for whisky to mature and means that those holding stocks of whisky not only have their money tied up for a long time, but they have to make an estimate of the potential market five or more years ahead. We shall shortly see that the peak year of 1978 was followed by a progressive decline which accounts for the overstocking which has created such a problem for the industry over the last few years. The situation is summed up in an article in the *Financial Times* of 9 February 1985 written by Lisa Wood: 'There is so much whisky maturing in Scotland today that if the industry stopped all production in its distilleries tomorrow, it would take more than a year to bring the level of supplies into line with forecasts for world-wide demand in the next few years.'

TRENDS BETWEEN 1971 AND 1983

The historical trend in world sales from 1971 to 1983 is demonstrated by the graph on p.170 (*DSWG*, 1984). The top line shows the rise in total sales up till 1978 and then the fall to the present time. The figures here are in million litres of alcohol (mla). The sale of bottled blended whisky almost precisely mirrors this trend. Bulk sales, which have their own significance, are more constant at a much lower level. The sale

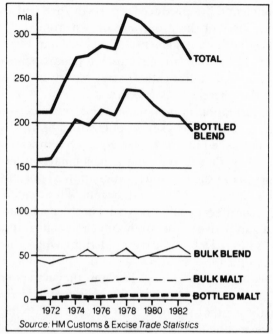

World sales of Scotch whisky by category, 1971–83 (*Distilling Sector Working Group Report*, 1984).

of bottled malt is right at the bottom and appears almost insignificant, but it has risen gradually over the years from just over 1 mla in 1971 to about 4.5 mla in 1983.

The *DSWG Report* (1984) notes a reduced rate of decline of the sale of blended Scotch whisky bottled in Scotland during the first six months of 1984. Exports of bottled malt increased by 25 per cent during this period, but it is emphasised that these half-year figures need to be assessed with caution. The overall trend seems obvious and we need to consider what might be responsible for it.

World recession is a dominant factor and if people have less to spend then the whisky trade is bound to suffer. A peculiar consequence of the successive oil crises is that the world's surplus disposable income has been directed to the teetotal Arabs and this has badly affected distillers (NF, 1984). Economic instability and shortage of foreign currency in many South American countries, which imported a good deal of whisky in the past, have resulted in a drop in sales. Venezuela is a case in point: sales of blended Scotch whisky fell from a peak of just under 10 mla in 1978 to just over 3 mla in 1983.

Drinking habits. A definite movement towards the drinking of white spirits and white wine has occurred in northern Europe and North America. A misleading impression that white wine contains less alcohol, and its relative cheapness due to a lower rate of duty, may be factors which have influenced this fashion. In the USA consumption of table wine has grown by four times over the past fifteen years and by 48 per cent in the last five years (*DSWG*, 1984). An increased interest in health and fitness has swept North America, and the UK is not far behind. Many people seem to feel that it is 'healthier' to drink white wine than spirits. This really is nonsense because it is the alcohol content not the nature of its vehicle which is important. It may be necessary to repeat the fact that a 12 cl glass of wine, at 11% vol, contains more alcohol than a pub measure of Scotch whisky.

There have been other changes in drinking in many countries which are less easy to explain, but they have, for the first time since the war, put Scotch whisky on the defensive in traditional key markets (*DSWG*, 1984).

Discriminatory tariffs. Many countries take a protectionist attitude towards the import of Scotch whisky and tax it more highly than locally produced spirits. For example, in Brazil in 1984, the tax on a bottle of Scotch whisky (75 cl, 43% vol) was £9.53, but the tax on local whisky was £0.69, and £0.20 on the lowest taxed local spirit. Similar figures for Japan were £5.62, £2.64, and £0.29. Even countries such as Sweden, which are trying to make drinking difficult and tax their local spirits high

(£8.36), have a tax of half as much again on Scotch. There are many highly technical fiscal and commercial problems all over the world and the SWA is very active in representing the interests of the whisky industry in many countries.

The opposition. Locally produced cut-priced whiskies present a threat to the market in Scotch whisky, as does the new fashion for cocktails and other 'mixer' drinks. Clearly it is important for the image of Scotch to be maintained, but concessions may have to be made to meet popular demand. For example, ready-mixed Scotch and soda, or even Scotch and lemonade or ginger, may be needed to meet competition from the ready-mixed gin and tonic which is now available.

Marketing methods seem to be regarded as the key to turn in order to reverse the down trend in sales. Advertising has been much more sophisticated during the last ten years or so and is much more attuned to the needs of the local markets. Presumably this is directly reflected by the way the brands which are popular in the USA are quite different from those that are popular in the UK. The market leaders in the UK in 1983 were Bell's, Famous Grouse and Whyte & Mackay; whereas in the USA the order was J & B Rare, Dewar's and Cutty Sark. But in world sales Johnnie Walker Red Label came first.

The *DSWG Report* (1984) concludes by recommending that the industry should seek every opportunity to promote the quality image of Scotch whisky in world markets and take all such measures as are necessary to *keep on the offensive.*

HIGH STOCKS

We have seen that the industry now holds large stocks of mature whisky. It clearly is a temptation for surplus stocks to be sold off cheaply and to be passed on to the consumer as an inferior blend. This is particularly likely to happen when there is a drive to lower prices in supermarkets and other retail outlets. Up to a point whisky gains in value the longer it is kept, so it is desirable that stocks should be dispersed gradually. The *DSWG Report* (1984) recommends 'that the industry continues to take all necessary steps first to bring, and then to keep, stock levels far more in line with anticipated demand.'

BULK EXPORTS

We have seen (p.170) that sales of bulk blend have remained constant overall, but there has actually been an increase in this form of export to the European Community countries. The *DSWG Report* (1984) feels that this is at the expense of 'Bottled-in-Scotland' Scotch whisky and is contrary to the long-term interest of the industry as a whole. One effect is certainly to reduce home employment in bottling and packaging.

The export of bulk malt is on a smaller scale but it could have unfortunate consequences, although there is some disagreement about this. The Chairman of the Distillers Company summed the situation up in the statement in the *Annual Report* for 1980:

We remain firm in our belief that the export of bulk malt whisky is damaging to the long-term interests of the Scotch whisky industry and we continue to take no part in this sector of the business. We are nevertheless concerned that the continuation and proliferation of this trade, actively encouraged in a number of important export markets where Governments have raised tariff barriers to support their large domestic grain spirit interests, is severely restricting the potential for blended Scotch whisky in those markets.

TAX

Ever since a tax was first levied on spirits in 1644, successive governments have found this a useful source of income.

The duty on a bottle of whisky was 6.5p in 1900, 57p in 1940 and £3.56 in 1980. The addition of Value Added Tax means that in 1985, the total tax on a bottle is between £5.65 and £5.72, at a time when an average blend would be bought for about £8.25.

The Chancellor of the Exchequer in his March 1985 Budget added only 10p to the duty payable (a tribute to the strength of the whisky lobby?) which was less than had been anticipated as judged by the cost of living index. Scotch is, however, taxed at a relatively higher rate than other alcoholic drinks. The SWA (1985) quotes the following figures for the amount of duty paid per centilitre of pure alcohol:

Scotch Whisky	15.77p
Sherry	8.86p
Beer	8.60p
Table Wine	8.17p

THE TRUE COST

We all grumble that whisky is too expensive and can blame the Government for adding to the cost. There are, however, other ways of looking at it. In an article in the *Listener* (4 April 1985) Dr Michael O'Donnell quoted some interesting figures: in 1938, a manual worker had to work 8½ hours to earn a bottle of whisky; in 1960, he earned it in 6 hours and by 1976, the time had dropped to 2½ hours. This reflects rising wages rather than cheaper whisky, but everything is relative. *Which?* magazine in February 1984 calculated that between 1963 and 1983, the price of a bottle of whisky had risen by 210 per cent compared with petrol which had increased by 655 per cent. During this period the retail price index had risen by 430 per cent and so had gas and the cost of entertainment. All these kinds of numbers can be interpreted in any way you want, but it might be that whisky drinkers haven't done so badly. Perhaps the price is now just about right?

THE FUTURE

It would be idle to try to predict the future for whisky after this very brief review, but all trade has its cycles. Since the beginning of this century whisky has been affected in a way which is reflected in the history of malt distilleries (Chapter 2). As in all other industries a great deal of rationalisation has been undertaken; for example, the closure or 'moth-balling' of malt distilleries. Some large organisations have diversified their interests within and outside the drinks industry, presumably hedging their investments, but it is satisfactory to know that smaller privately owned companies are surviving the storm.

Clearly the industry will have to bend and adapt to the changes which will occur during the remaining years of this century. There is every reason to believe that the adjustments being made will allow the industry not only to survive, but also to be ready to take part in the economic upturn when it comes.

It is to be hoped that the small, but important, trade in bottled malt whisky will be allowed to prosper and that the high standard of blended whiskies will be maintained in spite of the difficulties which exist at the present time.

Bibliography

Amis, Kingsley, 1972. *On Drink*, Jonathan Cape, London.

Barnard, A., 1887. *The Whisky Distilleries of the United Kingdom*, Harper, 1877; reprinted 1969 by David & Charles, Newton Abbot.

Birnie, William, 1937 and 1964. *The Distillation of Highland Malt Whisky*, Private.

Collinson, Francis, 1979. *The Life and Times of William Grant*, Wm. Grant & Sons Ltd.

Cooper, D., 1978 and 1983. *The Century Companion to Whiskies*, Century Publishing, London.

Cooper, D. and Godwin, F., 1982. *The Whisky Roads of Scotland*, Jill Norman & Hobhouse Ltd, London.

Daiches, D., 1969. *Scotch Whisky*, André Deutsch; & 1983, Fontana.

Dunnet, Alastair, 1953. *The Land of Scotch*, Scotch Whisky Association.

Forbes, K. J., 1948. *A Short History of the Art of Distillation*, Brill, Leiden.

Gardiner, Leslie, 1985. *The NB : The First Hundred Years*, Forth Studios Ltd, Edinburgh.

Gunn, Neil, 1935. *Whisky and Scotland*, Routledge, London.

House, J., 1976 and 1983. *Pride of Perth*, Hutchinson Benham, London.

House, J., 1972. *The Spirit of the White Horse*, White Horse Distilleries Ltd.

Laver, James, 1958. *The House of Haig*, John Haig & Co Ltd.

Lockhart, R. Bruce, 1959 and 1967. *Scotch*, Putnam, London.

MacDonald, Aeneas, 1930. *Whisky*, Porpoise Press, Edinburgh.

Morrice, Philip, 1983. *The Schweppes Guide to Scotch*, Alpha Books, England.

Moss, M. S. & Hume, J. R., 1981. *The Making of Scotch Whisky*, James & James, Edinburgh.

Murphy, Brian, 1978. *The World Book of Whisky*, Collins, London & Glasgow.

Ross, James, 1970. *Whisky*, Routledge & Kegan Paul, London.
Scotland's Distilleries, 1984. *An Illustrated Visitors' Guide*, Famedram Publishers, Scotland.
Sillet, S. W., 1965. *Illicit Scotch*, Beaver Books, Aberdeen.
Simpson, Bill, et al, 1974. *Scotch Whisky*, Macmillan, London.
Spiller, B., 1984. *The Chameleon's Eye*, James Buchanan & Co Ltd, London and Glasgow.
Wilson, Neil, 1985. *Scotch and Water*, Lochar Publishing.
Wilson, Ross, 1959. *Scotch Made Easy*, Hutchinson, London.
Wilson, Ross, 1963. *The House of Sanderson*, William Sanderson.
Wilson, Ross, 1973. *Scotch: its History and Romance*, David & Charles, Newton Abbot.

Articles, Reports and other publications

'Alcohol Abuse', Michael O'Donnell, *Listener*, 4 April 1985.
Annual Review, Scotch Whisky Association, 1983.
'Buying Drinks', *Which?*, Consumers' Association, December 1979.
'Can Malt Whisky be Discriminated from Blended Whisky?', S. Chadwick, H. A. F. Dudley and others, *British Medical Journal*, 24–31 December 1983.
'Distilled Spirits Survey', Nicholas Faith, *Economist*, 22 December 1984.
DCL Distillery Histories Series, Brian Spiller, 1981–3.
'Drink', *Which?*, Consumers' Association, October 1984.
Harrods Book of Whiskies, *Decanter*, 1984.
The Image Men get to Work', Lisa Wood, *Financial Times*, 9 February 1985.
Scotch in Miniature, Alan Keegan, Famedram, 1982.
Scotch Whisky: Questions and Answers, Scotch Whisky Association, 1969.
Scotch Whisky in the 80s, Distilling Sector Working Group, HMSO, 1984.
Statistical Report, Scotch Whisky Association 1984.
'The Water of Life', Wallace Milroy, *House and Garden*, January 1985.

In addition, almost all of the whisky companies have been good enough to send me publications on their history and current activities. Information has also been gained from a number of articles in *The Times* during 1985.

Index